Management for Beginners

The Ultimate Guide

for First Time Managers

M. J. Pontus

ISBN: 978-1-7397389-1-4

Management for Beginners

TABLE OF CONTENTS

Management for Beginners

INTRODUCTION

Most employees dream of climbing the corporate ladder. The first stop you make on this journey is becoming a manager. Whether you have been promoted from within an organisation or hired in a management role, it is quite thrilling. All those long hours at work and cancelled weekend plans have at last paid off. Take a moment to appreciate your journey. As exciting as this is, it also brings a significant change.

The new job role you have got means additional responsibilities, increased expectations, and plenty of extra work. You will now need to play several roles, day in and day out. This is one reason new managers struggle. It can also be a source of great stress. The idea is to avoid getting caught up in all the stress and find a way out. The good news is that you have an opportunity to get a head start. If you don't want this happiness to be short-lived, you must understand your new role's different challenges and responsibilities.

Managing different employees, overseeing their performance, implementing and developing different strategies for better management, conflict resolution, and managing yourself are some areas you are now expected to deal with. You need to demonstrate your capabilities and ensure the results desired are being reached. To do this, you need to understand what it means to become a manager.

Apart from managerial responsibilities, there are several other factors you should focus on. You need to ensure that your team is working as a cohesive unit to reach team goals and that you are all on the same page. Every organisation has several departments, and each department has different teams. As a manager, it is your primary responsibility to ensure the departments contribute to organisational growth and development. You are essentially the link between corporate and the employees. Therefore, the role you play is vital to the organisation.

The first step toward this is to learn what it means to be a manager. It becomes easier to take steps in the right direction by gathering all the knowledge and information you can. This helps ensure you reach your personal goals while leading the team toward success. Are you wondering how you can do all this? Well, this book is the perfect fit for you!

In this book, you will learn about everything you need to become an efficient manager. It offers information about different managerial styles and how to choose one, attributes of a brilliant manager, tips to build your reputation, and seamlessly transition into the new role. Once you understand all of this, it teaches you to become an effective communicator and coach your team to success.

As a manager, you are the coach, mentor, motivator, and trainer for your team members. Instructing and explaining, mentoring and coaching, motivating and inspiring, and delegating and supporting are vital roles you will play as a manager. The different tips and helpful advice given in this book will help you become better at all of this. It also teaches you about task delegation, positively influencing your team, and preventing burnout and disengagement. You will also be introduced to practical and straightforward suggestions to improve the chances of team success. Everything you need, from building team dynamics to socialising with the team and managing remote employees to making positive changes, is presented in this book. Learning to manage internal politics, dealing with negative attitudes at the workplace, and managing different personality types are some unwritten responsibilities of a manager. Once you are armed with the information given in this book, doing all this will become easier.

Apart from all these topics, this book also deals with human resources and strategies you can use to resolve conflicts, write job descriptions, discipline employees, hire, interview, and fire people, and employee appraisals. There are several roles a manager has to play. As a new manager, it is your responsibility to ensure that your team is working in the right direction and attaining its objectives as expected. Unless you are aware of all the roles you will play, accomplishing these goals becomes difficult. Besides managing your team and acting as a link, you need to pay attention to another aspect of your life: yourself. Managing yourself is critical for your professional growth and development. In this book, you'll learn about self-management, tips to increase personal discipline, enhancing your emotional intelligence, preventing burnout as a manager, and being the best version of yourself.

This book will act as your guide every step of the way. You don't have to worry as a new manager because everything you need has been discussed in great detail in this book. All you need to do is spend some time and carefully go through the information it contains. Once you are armed with this information, making better decisions becomes simpler. This book contains additional information you might not have been introduced to in business or management courses!

So, are you eager and excited to learn more about all of this? Do you want to be the best manager you can be? If yes, let's get started without further ado.

CHAPTER 1: WHERE TO START

Managers play a crucial role in any organisation, regardless of its size. They are responsible for leading employees within a specific department to attain organisational and departmental goals. Managers essentially act as the communication channel between the executive team and all the employees who work under them. As is evident from the name, the primary role of a manager is to manage the team members they trusted to oversee. Managers also act as a middleman between customers and organisations, help equip the employees with skills required to complete the project, conduct performance reviews, hire employees, maintain and track the results and department budgets, and make decisions on behalf of the department.

Choosing A Managerial Style

Selecting a managerial style is crucial because it determines the level of engagement with the employees. So, what does a management style mean? It essentially refers to how a manager works to attain goals. Planning, organisation, decision-making, the delegation of responsibilities, and staff management are all a part of the management style. The management style depends on various factors, ranging from the company's hierarchical order to the control level and the manager's personality. An efficient manager is flexible enough to make the required changes to managerial style to ensure optimum output and work efficiency.

Several internal and external factors influence the management style. Some internal factors include the organisation's policies and objectives, employee engagement and retention, employees' skills, and the corporate or organisational culture. Depending on the employees' skill levels, the degree of management and supervision is required to attain the desired objectives and changes. Some external factors include competitors, employment laws, financial conditions, and consumers. Even though these factors are beyond one's control, they affect the organisational policies and, in turn, the managers.

Management Styles

There are different managerial styles and unless you choose one, leading your team to success becomes tricky and unnecessarily challenging. The wrong management style can hurt everyone in the organisation and even reduce organisational efficiency. An improper management style lowers team engagement. There are different drawbacks to using an unsuitable managerial style, from lower productivity and poor work quality to increased turnover of employees and reduced profitability. Remember, the manager and the team need to work together as a unit to achieve departmental and organisational objectives. If there is no cohesion at this level, it demotivates employees. It can also encourage them to leave the organisation in extreme cases.

In this section, let's look at some desirable and undesirable management styles.

Visionary Style Of Management

In this management style, the manager essentially communicates the purpose or the direction the team or employees should be heading. This, in turn, prompts the team to work harder to execute the said vision. Once the team's vision is set and a strategy to get it is established, visionary managers allow team members or employees to work on their terms. As long as the employees are productive, their methods aren't a concern to the manager. Instead, merely check in on the team to ensure they are working on the right vision and are on the right track.

This style of management provides a sense of autonomy for managers. This autonomy fulfils a basic psychological need for self-direction that all humans have. When you feel more in control of a situation, it increases the desire to work toward it. By allowing your team members' inner motivations to guide how they want to accomplish a task, their overall engagement increases. These managers are stern and fair. Even if they have already established a vision, they always listen to their team members' ideas and suggestions. They are flexible enough to make changes as and when required.

Visionary managers offer plenty of feedback to their teams about their performance. Whenever the team's performance meets their expectations, they don't shy away from praising and rewarding. The only factor you need to remember here is to sell your vision or idea to your team members before expecting them to execute it. If you inspire and get them excited about your vision, it becomes easier to achieve it.

Democratic Style Of Management

In a democracy, the majority always wins. This is the same rule that democratic managers use. Team members or employees are not excluded from the decision-making process, and instead, they're allowed to be a part of it. A democratic manager appreciates the team's diversity and ideas and understands their team members' importance. Even though the manager ultimately approves all decisions, the employees are involved in this process. By doing this, employees feel more engaged in the overall outcome.

It helps forge a healthy relationship between managers and the team. Whilst the managers develop the goals by involving the employees in this process, their shared morale increases. Since the employees are involved in this process, any decision the team makes is theirs, too. This sense of contribution and belongingness makes it easier for the manager to sell the team's vision to all the employees who execute it.

This is perhaps one of the most common styles of management. It also teaches the employees and team members a sense of responsibility while allowing them to make the most of their potential. On the downside, it leads to inefficient management when executed poorly. If you keep overthinking every decision even after consulting the entire team or cannot reach a decision, it slows down the entire process. If you want to follow this management style, you need to be a good leader. Learn to make decisions while being a good listener.

Transformational Style Of Management

Innovation is the keyword in this form of management. Transformational managers realise that change and growth are inevitable to help the team stay ahead of the curve. They continuously push their team members to do better and step outside their comfort zones to attain this purpose. By doing this, the manager is essentially helping the team discover their potential while raising the bar for better performance. When the team members realise they are more capable than they initially thought, the internal motivation to do better increases.

Transformational managers have an inherent belief that they can help their team members attain that true potential by continually challenging and motivating them. This essentially makes the team more dedicated and happier in the work environment. If you want to follow this managerial style, you need to be there by your team's side and help them whenever required to attain the group objectives. These teams are more adept at getting acclimatised to changes. On the downside, the team might end up spreading themselves too thinly or move too quickly. Unless you are constantly prepared to challenge the existing status quo, you cannot facilitate innovation within the team. It is also essential to understand when you shouldn't push your team. If you force them too much, you risk burning them out, which helps no one.

The Coaching Style Of Management

As the name suggests, those who opt for this management style are like sports coaches. They try to help their employees work toward professional development. These managers thrive by teaching their teams to do better and watching them grow in stature as individuals within the organisation. As long as they know they can get better results in the future, they are good at dealing with their employees' failures.

Coaching managers often use professional development opportunities to motivate their team members. Whether it is added responsibilities at work or the chance of promotion, these rewards encourage their teams to do better. It also helps the team members increase their existing knowledge and skill set. When you are focused on teaching your employees new things and providing valuable career opportunities, it becomes easier to establish stronger bonds within the team.

On the downside, this form of management could result in a toxic work environment. If you want to follow this managerial style, it is essential to oversee your team's personal development while bringing them together as a cohesive unit.

Now, let's look at some styles to avoid.

Autocratic Style

In this type of management style, communication is often one way and always flows down from the top-level management to the employees. It is essentially a top-down approach. In the autocratic style, all the decision-making power lies with the management, and this leadership style is believed to be one of the most controlling managerial types. Employees need to be closely monitored while performing their duties within clearly defined parameters.

Instead of motivating their team by offering rewards or scope for personal and professional development, autocratic managers use shame, fear, and guilt to get the job done. These managers favour micromanaging. Micromanagement leaves little room for flexibility and growth. The employees governed by such managers need to do what they're told. Also, they aren't given a chance to offer feedback. The lack of innovation, inherent motivation and the desire to do better are some drawbacks of this management form. When a few people handle all the decision-making, it results in stagnation. The lack of innovation reduces the scope for growth and development. When the employees are not given a chance to take part in decision-making, it reduces their inherent desire to do better. This is an incredibly ineffective style of management. Even the most skilled employees are not given a chance to showcase their talent or potential.

The only time this management style comes in handy is when the organisation or the team is in a crisis. When important decisions need to be made quickly, the autocratic management style is favourable.

Servant Managers

Managers who follow this management style prioritise their team and employees' wellbeing more than their results do. The primary aim is to establish and maintain harmonious relationships with all their employees and keep them happy. Therefore, most of their activities and decisions support the team members. In return for their support and encouragement, they expect their employees to work hard and stay motivated.

On the downside, these managers give little importance to employees' performance and shy away from any confrontations. Even if the employees' performance is subpar, they don't pressure them to work more efficiently. This results in a complacent work culture that doesn't produce any significant results. When all the time, attention, and resources go toward team building and bonding instead of work, attaining goals and objectives becomes difficult. It can become quite frustrating for performance-driven employees.

Laissez-faire Style Of Management

This is a hands-off approach to management. Even though the managers monitor all their team's activities, they don't take a proactive approach to check in with their team members or offer them help and support when required. Instead, they work expecting their team will perform according to pre-establish levels of expectations. The decision-making authority lies in the hands of the team members. They are free to work, but they want as little intervention from the managers as possible. This autonomy might sound like a genuinely lovely perk, but it can lead to discord and chaos. The team members are free to reach out to the manager if they need any help.

On the downside, the team rarely has any sense of group vision or goals. Apart from this, the manager's lack of proactive guidance means they are often pulled in various directions. Therefore, the team's overall productivity reduces in this managerial style. When the managers at different levels don't show any active involvement, it can make the team members and employees feel somewhat neglected. This is not an effective style of management and is believed to be among the least desirable ones.

Transactional Style Of Management

In this managerial style, the managers use various rewards and incentives to motivate their team members to get things done. This is quite similar to bribery. The message conveyed is that the employees will get something if they do something in return. Using extrinsic motivation can be helpful, but this is not a long-term strategy. After all, only so much inspiration, an employee will feel about obtaining rewards or incentives such as bonuses and stock options before their intrinsic motivation reduces.

Also, it is essential to remember that the work environment and culture are steadily changing these days. Employees are no longer motivated by the thought of extrinsic rewards. Instead, they are looking for personal value, growth, development, and so on. The transactional style of management cannot fulfil these objectives. Intrinsically motivated employees perform better and show a positive attitude toward the work. It can also reduce the team's engagement toward obtaining their collective goals and objectives. Apart from this, the transactional management style doesn't emphasise the importance of the team's cohesiveness. Instead, it places too much emphasis on whether the team carries out the manager's commands or not. Without decision-making authority, the team's engagement reduces and creates discord in relationships between the team and the manager.

If your goal is to improve team productivity and work quality, you need intrinsically motivated team employees.

Now that you know the different management styles, note which one works well for you. Once you better understand the team members or employees you manage, change your management style according to circumstances. Therefore, it would be better to keep an open mind and adopt a flexible management approach.

Here are some links you can use to self-assess your management style.

http://bit.ly/management-style-quiz

http://bit.ly/leaders-style

Attributes Of A Great Manager

Now that you're aware of different managerial styles, it's time to be the best manager you can be. To do this, you need to be mindful of the other qualities and attributes an excellent manager should have. These attributes make all the difference between creating a happy, intrinsically motivated, and highly productive team that attains its objectives and goals and one that doesn't.

In this section, let's look at some attributes that all managers should have.

Creating Mutual Trust

Every relationship is based on some form of trust or mutual respect. Without mutual trust, no relationship can exist. If your team members don't feel safe or secure enough to openly communicate their ideas, opinions, worries, or even hesitations, it creates an unfavourable work environment. It is okay to avoid all possible mistakes. At the same time, you need to avoid creating an environment that condemns all errors. A productive team knows and understands that mistakes are a part of the road map toward success. If you crucify your team for all their mistakes, failures, or misunderstandings, it creates a toxic manager/employee relationship.

Concentrate On The Strengths Of Your Team

Creating a workplace based on strengths is crucial if you want to enhance your team's performance. This essentially means you need to spend some time understanding your team members' and employees' different strengths and skills. This is time well spent on managing a team. Unless you know what your employees are good at, you cannot delegate responsibilities to the right team members. By understanding their strengths, you get a better idea of the roles they are best suited for. When the employees know their personal growth and development are valued, they are naturally motivated to do better.

Avoid Micromanaging

Regardless of what you do or the managerial style you opt for, there's one thing you must avoid at all costs, and that is micromanaging. Micromanaging your team reduces their overall productivity and creates discord. It can also harm the relationship you have cultivated with your team members. A successful leader and manager know not to obsess over every detail, decision, and action the team takes. If you want your team to succeed, avoid micromanaging. It is quite tempting to believe that you have better control over the outcome by guarding every detail. Instead, it has the opposite of the desired effect. It can make your team feel too controlled. It also takes away any scope for personal development. Micromanagement reduces employee motivation and initiative to do better. Once you have delegated responsibility, you can check in from time to time to ensure they are on the right track and offer help when required. Apart from this, refrain from constant check-ins.

Learn To Be Assertive

Learning to be assertive is a valuable trait in all aspects of your life. This is an essential skill for all managers. When you are assertive, it shows you believe in the idea and will back it up. Assertiveness also naturally puts you in the leader's role. Your team needs to understand that you are the leader, and they need to follow your directions. That said, it is important to temper your assertiveness with empathy and diplomacy. Assertiveness helps overcome any resistance and increases the employee's internal drive for success. If you are not assertive, it reduces the team's confidence in you and your abilities. If you seem unsure of the plans you propose, why would your team follow your example?

Employee Development Matters

Concentrating on employee development and training is essential if you want your team to grow and prosper. Identifying different areas, skills, and opportunities to help employees learn and master new skills increases team strength and confidence. Suppose there are no growth or developmental options available for an employee, their desire to work better decreases. When you concentrate on employee development, it conveys a vital message that you are concerned about their wellbeing and are actively working toward it. By making your employees feel valued, you increase their motivation to work better.

Learn To Handle The Pressure

As a manager, you will continuously face stressful situations. Unless you learn to deal with these situations properly, you cannot set a good precedent for your team. After all, your team looks up to you in times of crisis. If you lose your calm, your team will lose its sense of direction. Regardless of how dire a situation seems, deal with this pressure properly. Don't let it get the better of you. Emotional stability is one of the essential traits of a manager. There will be days when it feels like you have a target painted on your back. You will be held accountable for your team's performance. You cannot shift the blame onto them at the last moment. By taking good care of yourself and positively dealing with work pressure, you can increase your team's productivity. Avoid getting overwhelmed and concentrate on managing your emotions.

Be Open

You need to keep an open attitude and mindset at work. A fixed mindset is detrimental to growth, development, and success in all aspects of life. Being a manager doesn't mean you always know the best. Accept this simple fact and keep an open mind. Be receptive to suggestions, feedback, and ideas your team offers. By doing this, you are essentially conveying the message that you value and respect your team and employees. This is important for their overall development and increases productivity.

Good Analytical Abilities

Apart from being good at communication, you need to have good analytical abilities. Your job is not just to ensure the team is working as a cohesive unit, but it is equally vital to ensure they are working in the right direction. Analytical abilities help make the most of the resources available at your team's disposal. It also gives you a chance to assign the right task to the right individual. Good analytical and cognitive abilities lead to better decision-making. By regularly analysing your team's work, you can identify areas where they excel and where there is scope for improvement. It also helps keep an open mind about different opportunities that present themselves.

Always Recognise Good Work

It is essential to push your team in the right direction by offering support, help, and guidance. If you are quick to criticise any mistakes they make, ensure you are equally adept at recognising and rewarding their good work. If you fail to do this, it creates a hostile work culture. It can reduce the team's morale to do better. Once the team starts believing they will not be recognised, or their hard work will not be rewarded, their motivation to do a better job will reduce. If you want to increase employee engagement while enhancing their overall productivity and loyalty toward the team and the organisation, learn to recognise and reward their excellent work. As a rule of thumb, always reward someone for their superb work in public, but have one-on-one conversations while criticising them.

Honest Communication Is Vital

The importance of communication can never be overlooked in any relationship. Assertiveness and honesty go hand in hand. If the team feels they cannot count on their leader to give them straight answers, it creates mistrust. The need for honest communication is essential to establish mutual trust. Don't choose diplomacy or hide behind a curtain of politeness while offering feedback. Strike a balance between courtesy, empathy, and honesty. Avoid compromising on one trait for the sake of the other. Honesty is the best policy and always live by it in your managerial role. If there are any developments or changes, communicate them with your team. While doing this, show some emotional intelligence and don't get overwhelmed.

Be A Good Role Model

As a manager, you are also the leader of the team. You need to set an excellent example if you want the team to improve themselves. Diligence, enthusiasm, open communication, assertiveness, and leadership are skills that all managers should possess. If you cannot model good behaviour, don't expect it from your team members.

It Is Not A Dictatorship

Becoming a manager means you need to be a good leader too. A good leader knows there is a difference between leading, managing, and dictatorship. It can be quite challenging to distinguish between controlling the environment and becoming a dictator. If you want to impact your team positively, ensure that you don't become a dictator. To do this, it is crucial to learn the difference between authoritarian and authoritative leadership styles. Do these terms sound similar? They are, in fact, significantly different. The autocratic leader lives by the "Do as I say" motto. This attitude creates a dictatorship, which is highly undesirable for your team's productivity and growth.

Authoritarian leaders cause general distrust and chaos within their employees. Their inability and absolute refusal to listen to anyone, especially those leading, create an undesirable work environment. Criticism doesn't go down well with such leaders, and all decisions are based on their ideas. Even if the team members have the required expertise and knowledge to make better decisions, an authoritarian manager will refuse to listen to their input.

Authoritative leaders work with their teams to achieve common goals. This is one of the most desirable styles of leadership in several circumstances. Even though the decision-making power lies in the manager's hand, they lead while listening to others' feedback. They are flexible enough to change the plan of action based on the team's needs and requirements or the changing circumstances. It is a more relaxed approach toward managing without compromising on assertiveness. These are the kinds of leaders that individuals want to follow. It helps increase their motivation and enthusiasm to do better.

Here are some tips you can follow to become an excellent manager while avoiding dictatorship.

Quickly Address Issues

Challenges, problems, and hurdles occur in every aspect of life. The same rings true in a business environment, too. Employees will disagree, have personal conflicts, and strategies might not work as expected. In such instances, an excellent manager knows when to step in and help the employees fix them. Instead of telling them to deal with their issues on their own or demanding immediate resolution, a good manager offers guidance.

If you don't want to be perceived as a dictator, you need to sit down and communicate with all involved. Try to identify what is happening and view the issue from the perspective of the involved individuals. You will never truly understand what went wrong unless you learn to do this. The lack of this crucial information increases the risk of similar circumstances repeating themselves in the future. When you look at a problem from an employee's perspective and seek feedback, it makes them feel valued and respected. Chances are when you indulge in this communication, you get better insight into the problem its reasons and discover how it can be prevented in the future.

Now, your job just doesn't end here. Once you have all the information you need, offer a suggestion based on the information you have got. Don't dictate commands and expect them to be followed blindly. Remember, you shouldn't be a dictator. As a manager, you need to manage, motivate, coach, and lead your employees. Also, don't forget to offer help with implementing suggestions and solutions. For instance, if you notice employees cannot meet deadlines because of added responsibilities, try to delegate some roles. You can improve their efficiency by taking a couple of tasks off their plate instead of expecting them to meet unrealistic targets.

Concentrate On The Team Culture

The most effective means of establishing a desirable workplace dynamic is building a good team culture. What does team culture mean? It essentially means understanding all the factors that make your team members or employees feel comfortable and supported in their roles. To build a good team culture, you need to think about the ideal workspace environment from the employee's perspective. How do you want your team members or employees to feel when they come to work daily? What can you do to achieve all this if you want more creativity, better innovation, and brilliant ideas? One of the most effective ways to do this is by rewarding your employees whenever they do any of these things. To do this, you need to have regular conversations, professional interactions, personal meetings, and brainstorming sessions with your team and with individual team members.

A dictator seldom pays attention to all this. It is quite simple to become an efficient manager without stepping into the role of a dictator. All it takes is a little emotional intelligence. If you want your team to prioritise and support each other and work toward obtaining team objectives while improving personal development, investing in team-building exercises is a good idea. Team-building activities help strengthen the relationships between individuals and the team as a whole. When everyone works as a cohesive unit, obtaining pre-established goals and objectives becomes easier. It also reduces any chances of unnecessary conflicts. A healthy team doesn't have any unhealthy competition between them.

Communication, Communication, Communication

If you don't concentrate on communication, you cannot create a healthy work environment conducive to individual employees' success and well-being. There needs to be open and honest communication between different team members. This ensures they can quickly and effectively communicate their ideas, suggestions, and opinions without worrying. It helps establish better interpersonal relationships. While you do this, you need to pay attention to another aspect of communication. Apart from the communication between team members, open and honest communication should exist between different management levels. Instead of giving your team members a phone number or an email address they can use to reach you, ensure sufficient time for face-to-face interactions.

As a manager, your team needs to understand that they can reach out to you whenever they need help. If you are unavailable, it creates mistrust and discord within the team. It can also eventually result in unnecessary resentment. Work on developing and implementing an open-door policy. When your team knows they can count on you, it shows mutual trust and understanding. If you establish any communication barriers, it creates a dictatorial form of management. When you play a dictator's role instead of a manager, it reduces the employee's motivation to work with you or even among themselves as a team. Ensure your behaviour and workplace environment encourage efficient communication.

Always Pay Attention To Your Team

As a manager and leader, paying attention to your team is a part of your job description. Always stay on top of things and get a better sense of what is going on in the workplace. If any conflicts or unacceptable behaviours harm the team dynamic, pay attention to those involved. Don't allow such problems to fester. Include more group thinking and engage your team. Don't be hesitant to reinforce and reward all positive and desirable behaviours. By establishing good group dynamics, it helps increase employee productivity and satisfaction. When your employees feel all this, their inherent motivation to do better increases; instead of becoming a dictator, concentrate on being authoritative and inspiring.

Build Trust And Confidence

As a manager, an important responsibility that lies on your shoulders is to build and maintain the trust and confidence of your team and employees. Without trust, you cannot establish productive relationships in any aspect of your life. It can even create a toxic work environment. Effective leadership is vital to establishing trust and confidence at work.

In this section, let's look at some simple tips and techniques you can follow to build trust and confidence as a new manager.

Own Your Mistakes

A common mistake many managers make is that they try to present themselves as the influential authority figure. They do this to show their position as a leader. It is vital to ascertain your leadership and authority, but remember not to go overboard. If you want to be a good leader and a manager, it is essential to teach your team about responsibility. Don't just take credit for when things go according to plan, but learn to take responsibility for any mistakes. Accepting your mistakes is a sign of self-respect and confidence. It also shows your team that they can trust you. When you own your mistakes, it makes it easier for your team members to accept the errors, too. Unless you do this, learning and growing can become difficult. Once you accept your mistakes, don't forget to make amends as well.

Invest In Others

A simple way to show that you believe and trust your employees is by investing in them. It shows they are valued if you help them develop the skills or give them opportunities for growth and development. Help your team members grow. When they grow, they become more motivated to do better. When they do better, improving team efficiency becomes easier. Investing in your employees serves a dual purpose by showing your willingness to direct organisational resources toward their development.

Their motivation to become contributing members of the team will increase.

Display Consistency

Remember, displaying consistency in your professional dealings shows you are trustworthy and reliable. It also helps earn the respect of your team and employees. It's important to talk the talk and walk the walk too. If you make any promises, make sure that you keep them. Don't be so eager to please your new team that you make promises that cannot be kept. You not only end up disappointing your team, but make them question your reliability too. It puts you in an awful situation, and there is no way you can come out of it looking like a winner. If you don't want to seem dishonest or incompetent, try to be realistic. Your team's confidence in you increases when you deliver on your promises. This is also a great way to build consistency.

Displaying consistency is crucial for all managers who want to earn the team's trust, respect, and confidence they need. Don't make the mistake of treating different employees differently. If there is a specific rule or guideline, ensure it applies to everyone. Take it a step further and ensure that you follow all the organisational rules and procedures, too.

Never Hesitate To Ask For Feedback

As human beings, we all have our vulnerabilities. To elicit trust and confidence, it is important to display your vulnerabilities. When the employees know you are aware of your vulnerabilities and weaknesses and aren't shying away from them, you seem more human. If you want your employees to work on their vulnerabilities, accept yours. The simplest way to do this is by seeking feedback from your team or employees. By doing this, you show no one is above criticism, and everyone needs to learn.

Delegate Responsibilities

Trust is not a one-way street. You need to show trust to be trusted. If you want your employees to trust you, show confidence in their abilities, too. The simplest way to do this is by delegating responsibilities. One important rule you need to remember while doing this is to avoid micromanagement. Once you have delegated responsibility, trust your employees to make the most of their capabilities to get things done. It doesn't mean you should not check on them or monitor their progress. Giving them more responsibilities shows you trust them and value their contributions to the team and organisation.

It can be quite tempting to do everything on your own. If you want to build trust in the workplace, avoid this. When you don't delegate, you prevent others from developing their skills. The struggle is vital for growth. This is where you step in as a manager. If you realise an employee is struggling with a specific task, offer the required help to complete it. Instead of doing it for them, give them a chance to learn and explore. If you don't do this, you are effectively stopping them from growing.

If you fail to delegate responsibilities, it shows you don't trust their abilities. It can seem like a personal attack on the employees. By concentrating on your team's self-empowerment, you increase the trust between the employees and the management. Rather than focusing on perfection, learn to help others grow. If there are mistakes, they can be fixed with a bit of help and guidance. After all, you are their coach, comment and guide, leader, and role model. If you don't model good behaviour, how can you expect it from others?

Always Lead By Example

The quickest way to lose the trust of your employees is by setting a poor example. For instance, if you want your employees to be punctual, regardless of whether it is attending a meeting or completing work, you need to be punctual too. Always practice what you preach. If you are not punctual but expect or demand punctuality from them, you are setting a poor example. Never assume a "Do as I say, not as I do" approach at work. If you don't follow your own rules, you cannot order them to follow you. It will certainly make them lose that trust in you.

Don't Forget To Express Your Gratitude

The importance of gratitude is crucial in all areas of life. While managing, follow the mantra of praising in public and criticising in private. Don't air your dirty laundry in front of other departments and employees. If there seems to be a problem within your team, solve it without alerting everyone. Publicly criticising your team members and employees will demoralise them and reduce their intrinsic motivation to work as a cohesive unit. Whenever your team does something well, don't forget to appreciate the job they have done. It's better to praise their efforts, even when they haven't achieved the desired results. If you know your employees have tried their best, but the results were unfavourable, embrace their efforts. If you don't, the employees will eventually develop a complacent attitude detrimental to growth and development.

Limit The Lectures

A common mistake many managers make is taking a keen interest in lecturing others. If you want your employees to make the right decisions, don't give in to the urge to continually lecture them. When you do this or always tell your team members what they should or should not do, it shows you have no faith in them. Eventually, it will erode their trust in you. After all, trust is a two-way. If you want your employees to trust you, learn to trust them. Even well-intentioned advice can backfire. Remember, no one likes unsolicited advice. Be there for your team when they need it. Also, avoid micromanaging. The importance of avoiding micromanaging cannot be stressed enough.

Instead of lecturing, it is better to ask reflective questions. Ask them what they think about a specific suggestion, idea, opinion, or solution. Prompt them to think further by suggesting an alternative without forcing them to implement it.

Be A Good Listener

Learn to be a good listener. Don't just hear what others say because you want to reply, but listen to learn what they are saying. Being a good listener is a great way to influence your employees and team members. It shows you value and appreciate what the other person is saying. It is also a sign of respect for someone else. If you want your team members to listen to you, you need to reciprocate.

If an employee says something, try to understand it from their perspective. Instead of evaluating and analysing whatever you hear from your point of view, step into their shoes. Don't be in a rush to respond and instead give them a chance to express themselves. By acknowledging your employees opinions and feelings, you are essentially building mutual trust and respect.

How To Transition Into The New Role

Most managers in an organisation are usually promoted from within the ranks. This is a significant achievement and a step in the right direction while climbing the corporate ladder. If you were just promoted to a managerial role, learning to transition into this new position is essential. You need to ensure this transition goes smoothly. How you handle yourself during this period shows a lot about your skills and potential. This also gives you a chance to prove your merit, especially if the old manager is still around. If you don't want any constant comparisons to be drawn between you and the previous manager, here are some tips you can use.

Let Go

Every role in an organisation is different, and it comes with varying responsibilities. Let go of all ideas and notions about your previous obligations. You cannot move on to your new position if you haven't let go of the previous one. Essentially, you need to keep an open mind and empty your cup. Concentrate on your new duties, roles, and responsibilities. Work on improving your existing skill set to cater best for your new role.

Listen And Observe

While you transition into your new role as a manager, it is essential to note all the changes you wished to see while working under a previous manager. Chances are, there may be particular ideas you want to implement or changes you want to see within the workplace. Well, if that's the case, it's better to introduce them gradually and not enforce them immediately. Remember, it's not just you who is getting used to the new role, as even your team and other employees need to get used to you. Give them a chance to get accustomed to all of this. If you implement significant changes immediately, it can throw your team off balance. It can also reduce their overall productivity and create internal discord. The idea is first to get them accustomed to your managerial position before bringing about any changes. Once you get the team's trust and confidence, it becomes easier to implement any change you wish to see.

Get To Know Your Employees

It is crucial that you truly understand your employees and team members. If you want to be approachable, this is the first step toward attaining that aim. Make a note of all the different things they like doing, their triggers, and their skills. Once you have a proper grasp of the team you manage, it becomes easier to delegate responsibilities and assign roles accordingly. Before you think about leading a team, get to know them. Whether it is a one-on-one session or a team lunch, concentrate on team-building activities. When you do this, you better understand your subordinates and recognise any managerial potential. As a leader and manager, you need to look for someone who can succeed you later.

Make Your Team Feel Valued

The simplest way to ensure your team feels valued is by listening to them. The importance of being a good listener cannot be stressed enough when managing others. People management is one of the critical activities a manager needs to undertake. Even asking a simple question such as, "What do you think about this?" or "How does this make you feel?" does the trick. Don't forget to give your team members and subordinates due to credit. Trust cannot be demanded. Instead, you need to cultivate it slowly and remember to praise those who come up with equally innovative ideas.

Don't Forget Your Managerial Position

A common mistake most new managers make is that they forget they are in a position of authority. It is okay to want to earn your team's confidence and respect. You might also be tempted to be friendly with them to build better relationships. It is okay to be friendly, but don't forget about professionalism. After all, you are in a position of authority, and others need to respect you. They shouldn't think of you as a pushover. Instead, they need to view you as a leader, coach, mentor, guide, and manager. You are the boss first. Don't allow personal relationships to affect your professional ones. Learn to be friendly and in order. Don't be afraid to show that you are the one in charge.

Talk About Your Goals And Vision

As a manager, you have a responsibility toward yourself and all those you manage. Therefore, it is essential to discuss and clearly define your goals and visions for all the employees you manage. Apart from this, you need to set specific goals for the team. Without proper goals or vision, the team loses its sense of direction. It can also result in misuse or misallocation of limited resources. Establishing goals is essential if you want to optimise your team's productivity. A simple acronym you can use to do this is SMART.

SMART is a technique of goal setting. It essentially stands for small, measurable, attainable, relevant, and time-bound goals. Every goal needs to fulfil all these conditions. Even if one of them is missing, the goal becomes unattainable. Setting clear and actionable milestones makes it easier to ensure your team moves in the right direction.

Don't Forget To Be Adaptable

It is important to establish goals, but leave some room for flexibility.

Several factors are well beyond your control. When you set goals, make sure there is room for all of this. If you are not flexible or adaptable, it creates a stagnant work environment. It can also result in the wastage of resources. Become a situational leader. There is no one size fits all approach when it comes to managing employees in an organisation. Depending on the external circumstances, be flexible enough to change your managerial style. Especially in crisis, you might need to make decisions all on your own. There will be times when you need to consider your team's opinion before making any decisions. Depending on what the circumstance or situation demands, change your managerial style.

Never Stop Learning

If you want to grow and succeed in life, you need to keep learning. Growth seldom occurs within one's comfort zone. If you're going to grow, never stop learning. By continually improving your skills, acquiring new skills, and working on your individual development, you are setting an exemplary role model for others. If you want your team to grow, you need to grow too. By continually learning, you can ensure that you are equipped with all the information to make significant decisions.

Shifting to a managerial position can be a little overwhelming. During the initial weeks of transition, regulate your emotions. Most of your time and effort may have been spent accomplishing tasks when you were just an employee. Now that you are a manager, the first thing you need to do is understand that you are responsible for managing others. You are no longer the centre of attention, and it is perfectly normal. You are responsible for your team and employees to ensure they are moving in the right direction. At the same time, concentrate on team-building activities to create better team dynamics. You will learn more about doing all these things in the subsequent chapters.

Humour And Its Pitfalls

A sense of humour can be used as an icebreaker. It can diffuse a tense situation. Humour can establish better bonds with your team members and within the team. That said, there are two sides to everything. Humour can be helpful, but it can also become a significant hurdle if misused.

In this section, let's look at certain do's and don'ts, which you must remember while using humour in a workspace. Remember, you are a manager and have a significant influence over other employees and team members. Unless you use this influence properly, you cannot get your team to accomplish anything.

Never Joke About Personality

You can laugh about a specific act, statement, or even a characteristic displayed by an employee or team member. While doing this, be wary of ridiculing someone's personality. Don't defame or ridicule another employee to refute their arguments. This is simply unacceptable in any setting, let alone a professional environment.

Vulgar Jokes Are Unacceptable

Vulgar, crude, and coarse jokes are not acceptable in any relationship. Whether in your personal or professional life, refrain from making such jokes. It shows a lack of refinement and poor culture. Using a vulgar sense of humour can provoke unnecessary conflict between superiors and subordinates. It will be problematic, so refrain from doing it. If you ridicule someone's personality, disregard their skills, underestimate their abilities, or lean toward unnecessarily sexual innuendo, it will land you in hot water.

Never Laugh At Involuntary Blunders

It might be quite funny to laugh at accidents and involuntary blunders, clumsiness, or forgetfulness of your employees and team members. Occasionally, it might be funny, but avoid such humour at the workplace as a rule of thumb. These jokes result in conflict with the manager and can hurt the sentiments of your team members. For instance, if you laugh at an older man who slipped and fell, it shows poor taste. It can also alter the perception of your team members and other employees toward you. Learn to differentiate between comic and funny. These two things are not the same.

If you want to point out something that you believe the employee is not conscious of, you can do it politely. There is no need to turn it into a joke. You might end up hurting the personal feelings of your employees.

Never Joke About Something That Cannot Be Fixed

It is never okay to laugh about certain things that are well beyond an individual's control. If a person cannot fix their problem, refrain from turning it into a joke. For instance, any humour associated with someone's physical weakness, unusual body proportions, pre-existing medical condition, or even unique names are unacceptable. You cannot ridicule employees for their empathy, sympathy, or love.

Don't Be The First One To Laugh At Your Jokes

Many wrongly assume they are genuinely funny and are the first to laugh at their jokes. Avoid doing this. Using humour can help create a positive work environment. While doing this, be mindful that you don't upsell a funny anecdote or claim that you are witty. Doing this tends to have the opposite of the desired effect. When a manager or any other executive, for that matter, starts laughing before ending the joke or immediately after, the comic effect is reduced. When you laugh at your jokes, it creates an environment where the employees feel forced to laugh with you. If you don't want to become an object of ridicule, be mindful of how you use humour at work.

Use Humour To Offer Friendly Criticism

One of the best uses of humour is providing friendly criticism. Please remember that the idea is not to punish or ridicule your team member or employee. If you aren't careful, an ill-timed joke can seem like mockery. This can seriously hurt your relationship with the said employee or team member. This can also strengthen a pre-existing complex or insecurity the said person might have. Mockery must never be used in the workplace. It triggers feelings of shame, humiliation, and builds resentment. While using humour to offer criticism, it needs to be mild and friendly. Remember, you are not punishing the employee, but are merely correcting the mistakes.

Learn To Accept Humour

If you are prepared to dole out witty remarks and laugh at others, prepare yourself for comebacks, too. Eventually, someone or other will end up making a joke about something you have said. In such instances, refrain from taking unnecessarily harsh administrative action. Instead of getting upset about it, learn to laugh at yourself. If you believe you cannot do this, don't make any jokes to start with. You can create a light and pleasant work environment without using humour too. If you know how to laugh at yourself, don't hurt others' sentimental feelings, and don't crack jokes in poor taste, you are in a safe zone. Don't condemn your team members for their sense of humour if you have created a culture based on this.

Don't be afraid that others might use their wit. Don't snub others when they are joking. Laughing can be an excellent form of self-defence. When you laugh at yourself, it shows others you are confident and self-assured. That said, learn where to draw the line too. It is okay to joke with your team members, but not establishing boundaries is not correct. After all, you are their manager and it is your responsibility to take care of them. If they take you for granted, it creates an imbalance in the power equation and status quo. This is undesirable.

Be Stern But Considerate

As a manager, it is vital that you learn to be stern while considerate. You cannot be too harsh, or it results in an autocratic style of management. Similarly, if you are incredibly courteous to your employees enforcing no consequences, it results in a "laissez-faire" approach. Neither of these styles is desirable in management. A good manager knows how to balance both these aspects without going overboard in either direction. Remember, you are a manager, and it is your responsibility to ensure your team's wellbeing while increasing their overall productivity. You also have the added responsibility to ensure they are working in the right direction and achieving the desired results.

Being stern doesn't mean you're not friends with your team members. It doesn't mean you bark commands and expect them to follow them blindly or accept them with no resistance. You need to be assertive about your decisions and present yourself as their superior without stepping on toes. If you don't want to cause internal chaos and discord within your team, learn to showcase your assertiveness. While doing this, temper it with a bit of consideration. Simple acts of care include regularly checking in with your employees to see if they need something. Offering help and guidance whenever they come to you is also an act of consideration.

Do you remember all the unique attributes discussed in the previous section about what an excellent manager needs to have? Try to imbibe those attributes, and you will be an exceptional manager who is considerate too.

CHAPTER 2: UNDERSTANDING THE ORGANISATION

In the previous chapter, I introduced you to different tips and suggestions to better understand management and where to start. Now that you have transitioned into your new role as a manager, it is essential to manage expectations at the workplace and understand your role in the organisation and the department. In this chapter, you will learn more about the organisation, organisational culture, and managing expectations.

Managing Expectations

There will be expectations that employees and other higher-ups will have from you as a manager. Unless you understand them, it becomes challenging to create a plan of action to fulfil them. Depending on the precedent set by a previous manager, these expectations will vary. It is therefore important to manage all of them. Ideally, you need to set them up as early as possible. Whether it is an unplanned event or the process of planning itself, it is always better to set certain expectations. Doing this makes it easier for everyone to understand what you will do and how you wish to work. Whether it is a communication channel or allocation of

43

responsibilities, it becomes easier to determine the direction you desire to work by.

While setting expectations, you must be honest and straightforward. There needs to be no ambiguity while doing so. The presence of ambiguity at this stage merely confuses. By clearly communicating what you can and cannot do, you convey how others can manage their expectations based on these conditions. It also reduces the risk of others expecting too much of you.

If there are any changes you wish to bring about in the department, you must communicate these changes immediately. The communication you send out needs to be clear and precise. Since communication is a vital part of management, you need to become an effective communicator. You will learn more about all this in the next chapter.

When it comes to setting expectations, you mustn't over-promise and fail to deliver. Whatever goals you set, they need to be realistic and achievable. If you cannot deliver, it merely takes away your credibility and trust. As a new manager, it is vital to earn your employees trust and confidence. Failure to do this at an initial stage sets the tone for the future.

While doing all this, do not go overboard and over-manage your expectations. It can be quite stressful when you worry too much about what others expect. Remember, every individual is different, and therefore, we all think differently. You are not responsible for fulfilling everyone's expectations. Instead, by following the tips mentioned above, managing them becomes easier. You don't have to view everything from everyone else's point of view. If it makes sense to you and you believe you can deliver it, it becomes easier.

Understand Your Role

As a manager, there are several roles and duties you will perform within an organisation. The simplest way to manage your expectations and those of others is by understanding the role you play.

In this section, let's look at the most critical functions of a manager in any organisation.

The Role Of A Figurehead

There are several symbolic and ceremonial duties managers perform. Whether it is welcoming official dignitaries and visitors to sign legal documents, these are all managerial functions. These interpersonal roles include very little serious communication and are often associated with deciding in matters that are not of great importance. That said, these decisions and routine communications are crucial for the department's smooth function or even the organisation.

The Role Of A Leader

This might sound obvious, but all managers are leaders within an organisation. They are in charge of a specific department and all the other employees who work within it. There are different leadership roles associated with a managerial position, from hiring to training and motivating or disciplining. The formal and functional authority granted to managers allows them to exercise their power to get the things mentioned above done. Managers also have an additional responsibility of leading their team in the right direction while ensuring maximum productivity.

The Role Of Liaising

As a leader, the manager needs to motivate, encourage, and communicate regularly with all the team members and employees. Apart from this, a manager is also responsible for coordinating the different activities performed by the team. Therefore, a liaison is an important role played by a manager. Liaising effectively means you need to interact with everyone within the organisation to ensure there is coordination. Apart from interacting with your team, you also need to interact with the higher-ups and ensure everyone is on the same page about the attained objectives. Managers might also need to secure information and favour from external sources. Internal and external liaising is a part of your job description.

The Role Of Monitoring

The manager is tasked with the responsibility of monitoring the team, environment, subordinates, and peers. You will receive plenty of information about internal and external events to better understand the company's internal environment. Whether it has viewed what your competitors do or learning skills to improve your competency, there's a lot you need to do. By doing all this, you get a better sense of what your team is doing. By monitoring the information flowing through the organisation, you can ensure optimal and effective communication. This helps reduce hearsay, speculation, rumours, and unnecessary gossip, which can impede effective communication.

The Role Of Disseminating Information

Managers play the role of an information disseminator within the company. You are responsible for collecting information from various sources and ensuring it reaches the right people. The information you receive, especially the confidential information your subordinates don't have direct access to, needs to be disseminated to them. If the right people don't have access to essential bits of information required to perform their jobs optimally, it will reduce their overall productivity. If you don't distribute information appropriately, unambiguously, or to the right people, it creates confusion and chaos. By effectively executing your role as a disseminator, you ensure transparency in the workplace.

The Role Of An Entrepreneur

As a manager, you need to play the role of an innovator and creator. Managers need to take an active approach in initiating new ideas, implementing changes, and so on. You cannot be passive and need to play the role of an entrepreneur. Your primary aim is to continually improve your department's performance and ensure its adaptability to the changing circumstances.

The Role Of Disturbance Handler

On the route to success, they will be several obstacles and disturbances you need to overcome. As a manager, it is your responsibility to ensure you handle all the disruptions effectively and efficiently. Taking corrective action is a part of your job description. Different disturbances you need to skilfully, carefully, and effectively tackle, include trouble from customers, discord among employees, or any other unforeseen circumstances.

The Role Of Resource Allocator

Resources are always finite, but their applications are infinite, so you must make the most of the resources available at your disposal. Resource allocation ensures that the right people have the right resources to complete their designated tasks optimally. Perhaps the most important resource you can ever allocate to your team is your time. Physical, human, and monetary resources need to be responsibly allocated, and this is the job of a manager. As a resource allocator, you need to create a schedule for completing tasks, design the financial budget, and create other branch marks to ensure the team moves in the right direction. When resources are appropriately allocated, it increases the overall efficiency and effectiveness of the team's results. Always have an open-door policy when it comes to communicating with your employees and subordinates.

The Role Of A Negotiator

Managers play the role of negotiators while negotiating deals and bargains with insiders and outsiders alike. You need to ensure your team gets all the resources and advantages they can use to get ahead. You might need to negotiate with your team and employees for better loyalty and commitment. Similarly, dealing with your peers includes integration, cooperation, and increased coordination. You might also need to negotiate with your higher-ups to ensure your team gets their due credit.

The Role Of A Spokesman

A manager represents the organisation or department to outsiders; whatever you say and do is a direct reflection of your department and the company. You also have the responsibility of transmitting the correct information in the desired fashion to others. This includes organisational action, policies, and plans. You have a responsibility to keep everyone in your unit and other superiors informed. As a liaison between your managers, team members, and outsiders, communicating accurate information between all these people is vital. You need to keep them informed about the financial performance, quality of output, and employee engagement.

Though a manager plays several roles, they are all interdependent and inseparable. You need to perform all these functions simultaneously and work on integrating them. These are not only the rules you expect employees to perform, but they are also expected of you.

Understand The Work Culture

Workplace culture might seem like quite a simple topic to observe and understand. On the surface, it includes obvious factors such as individuals' behaviour, the general communication tactics and language used between peers, and the office layout. Still, there is so much more to work culture than all this. Organisational culture is the amalgamation of complex behaviours, values, reward systems, and procedures that comprise your organisation. The behaviour and enthusiasm of all employees within an organisation and the physical space give you a feel of the work culture.

A positive sign of efficient and desirable work culture is that the employees who work are genuinely interested in working in the organisation and are engaged with the tasks they perform. By taking some time to understand the existing work culture better, you can determine its current engagement levels. By understanding this, you can take measures to improve. Here are some simple tips you can use better to understand your organisation's working culture and your department.

The simplest way to understand the work culture is to talk to the people who make it. All it takes is a genuine and heartfelt conversation with your subordinates and employees to understand what matters to them. The funny thing about work culture is that its true nature is defined by everything that happens below the surface. Therefore, before you believe you know everything there is to know about the workplace culture, talk to your employees and team members. By asking them direct and open-ended questions, you can find out more about what they like and don't like about the organisational culture.

By analysing how your team works together as a unit, you get a better sense of how employees interact with one another and the existing work culture. Regular analysis of your team's work offers a better understanding of what works well and what doesn't. If you realise there is some scope for improvement, and chances are you will come to this realisation, you can take corrective action immediately.

As a manager, you need to play the role of a listener and an observer. It is not only important to get feedback and information from your employees and team members, but you should also observe whatever happens. What is happening around you in the department? How do other leaders interact with their team members? How do the senior managers interact with their middle managers and employees? How do these interactions sound the same to you? Are there any apparent conflicts that exist? How can the disputes be resolved? Whenever you observe and analyse everything, ensure that you are not judgmental or don't make any assumptions. Once you have all this information, it becomes easier to create a positive work environment.

By creating a positive work culture, you promote employee engagement. When the employees are engaged in the work they perform, their productivity will improve. It also reduces employee turnover while increasing that motivation to improve their output.

CHAPTER 3: COMMUNICATION IS THE KEY

Communication helps with self-expression and our ideas, thoughts, opinions, and so on. The importance of effective communication within an organisation cannot be overlooked. This is one of the added responsibilities every manager has on their shoulders. Effective communication helps improve the team's performance, overall productivity, cohesiveness, and attitude. Without mastering verbal and nonverbal communication skills, you cannot be an efficient manager. Every interaction you have with an employee is an opportunity to create a positive impact required to improve their overall performance.

Before learning about improving your communication skills, it is crucial to understand the different benefits they offer. All managers are tasked with the duty of providing regular feedback to their employees and teams. The input is based on their overall performance, behaviour, and output. This feedback directly affects how the employee or the team will perform and behave in the future. If the feedback you offer is exceptionally harsh, is not conveyed properly, or is ambiguous, it will directly affect their morale, behaviour, and output.

Managers are responsible for their teams and the link between employees, others in the managerial hierarchy, and different departments. Effective communication helps ensure one department communicates appropriately with another. An organisation is an amalgamation of several departments that work together as a seamless unit to attain organisational goals. If these departments don't communicate with one another, it will become increasingly challenging to achieve the set objectives. An added responsibility of managers is to communicate with employees in other departments to exchange information and ideas. Excellent communication skills help to establish trust, confidence, and mutually respectful relationships.

Conflict resolution is a crucial duty of all managers. When two or more people work together, conflict creeps in eventually. Unless you learn to resolve this conflict correctly, it can affect the overall productivity of the team. You will learn more about this in the following chapters.

Communication Styles

As a manager, you need to manage various team communication styles if you want to be successful. Everyone has a different way of communicating, and unless you navigate these differences, you cannot make the most of their skills. You get a better understanding of your employees and how you can work with them by understanding different communication styles. Communication is a skill we hone and develop throughout our lives. Therefore, it is crucial to understand what you should and should not do as a manager while using each of the communication styles discussed in this section.

Assertive Communicator

As the name suggests, these communicators are quite assertive and have high self-esteem. This is one of the best communication styles that you can deal with or use at work. These individuals do not lean toward passive or aggressive communication. Instead, they know how to present their case confidently without pushing others to the limits or resorting to manipulation. The idea is to attain their objectives, causing no harm to others. If they like something, they will directly approach and ask the concerned person about it. Even if they don't get what they want, they are the last ones to get upset about it and throw a tantrum.

While dealing with such communicators, it is important that you are straightforward and open with them. Don't forget to discuss any problems associated with them or their method of work. While doing so, you can expect them to be good listeners and pay attention to all you say. Avoid wasting their time, showing disrespect while they are expressing themselves, and interrupting them while communicating. Two-way communication is of paramount importance.

Aggressive Communicator

Aggression seldom gets anything done in life. The ones who resort to using this communication style are all about winning and everything that comes with it. They have an inherent belief that all their ideas, thoughts, opinions, needs, and emotions are better than those of others. Because of this, they can seem quite hostile and aggressive. They might even seem threatening. These communicators are pretty brash and abrasive. Others can feel intimidated when they are subjected to such abrasive interaction. These communicators don't value the concept of personal space and are constantly invading the personal spaces of others around them. It can make others feel quite uncomfortable and defensive. Even if the aggressive communicator's message is well intended, their delivery method often takes away the meaning associated with it.

While dealing with such communicators, you mustn't beat around the bush and immediately focus on the discussion topic. Expect scrutiny or criticism and be prepared to answer them on the spot assertively. Another expectation you can have while dealing with such communicators is bluntness and decisiveness. There are three things you should not do while dealing with such individuals. Never make any promises you think you cannot deliver. Do not take their decisiveness or bluntness personally and don't expect them to strike a friendly conversation about their personal life.

Passive-Aggressive Communicator

Even if some individuals are passive externally, their communication stems from aggression. Since they operate under a constant sense of internal anger, they tend to feel powerless. This can make them resentful and encourage the risk of engaging in sabotaging behaviours. From an emotional perspective, these communicators often seem sarcastic and patronising. They are the ones who operate the gossip mill and don't mind engaging in rumours. They are also bound to complain and sulk if they don't get whatever they desire. Don't be fooled by their calm demeanour. Even if they seem incredibly pleasant in person, their true feelings are often hidden. This can create quite a toxic environment if communication tactics are not changed.

While dealing with such individuals, it is essential to identify the message they are trying to communicate and concentrate only on the core issue or the problem and nothing else. Try to understand the causes of their unpleasant behaviour and whether you are a part of it. Another rule you must remember while dealing with such individuals is to set specific ground rules about basic communication. Whenever you are up against a passive-aggressive communicator, avoid taking their passive-aggressiveness personally. Do not let your emotions get the better of you and show some emotional intelligence. Do not respond passive-aggressively, and instead, try to stay calm.

Manipulative Communicator

Manipulation is seldom desirable in any aspect of life. Manipulative communicators rarely mean what they say. Instead, they try to develop various tactics, schemes, and techniques to influence others to get what they want without directly asking for it. Before others even realise what is happening, the manipulator has already trapped them. Manipulation takes away an individual's sense of free will and the power to decide. Manipulative communicators can be patronising and insincere. This behaviour can frustrate others. They are also adept at making others feel guilty for feeling frustrated. They operate by making others believe they are obligated to help them achieve their objectives.

While dealing with manipulative communicators at work, it is vital to recognise them. Unless you identify them, you cannot stay on guard and prevent them from getting the best of you. While doing this, remind yourself that their manipulation stems from fear or other repressed emotions. Before you meet such a person, ensure that you are aware of the agenda and stick to it at all costs. Don't forget to ask direct questions and talk about expected and desirable behaviours. If you are unsure of how to handle such an employee at work, consult your higher-ups.

As mentioned, they are adept at manipulating others' emotions, depending on their needs and requirements. Therefore, avoid getting embroiled in any form of emotional argument with such individuals. Do not give in to the urge to respond to their negative statements or criticism. Another tip you must remember is that you are the one in charge and should not let others push you around. If you realise a specific employee is targeting another for no apparent reason, reassign their responsibility and take the required steps to put this to an end. Once an outcome has been reached, discuss the organisational policies with the HR Department.

Submissive Communicator

These individuals detest conflict in any aspect of their lives and want to make everyone happy. Since they hate confrontations and conflicts, they go out of their way to avoid them. Therefore, they prioritise everyone else's needs instead of their own. It is relatively easy to identify such communicators in your team. They are the individuals who often apologise for expressing their opinions. When others decide for them, they are happy because they give away their sense of control.

They have a tough time expressing their feelings because they worry that any difference in opinions will lead to a confrontation or conflict. Since these things are undesirable for them, they try to avoid them at all costs. Even if they have good ideas, opinions, or suggestions, they will keep all these things to themselves. Their lack of self-confidence shows through their communication style.

While dealing with such individuals, ensure that you give them space and time to let their guard down and openly share their ideas. Don't forget to be patient and carefully listen to all their thoughts. Do not confront them or become angry immediately, but instead, talk to them slowly and calmly. Whenever such individuals communicate, please resist the urge to speak over them or interrupt their thought train. Never dismiss their opinions or suggestions as undeserving or invalidate them. Try to support their ideas and decisions whenever possible. With a bit of external support from the manager, such employees can overcome their submissiveness.

Social Media Work Group

The most common communication forms within an organisation include emails, text messages, phone calls, and personal meetings. Apart from all this, there's another form of interaction that is steadily gaining popularity, and it is social media. Communication has become easier than ever through social media. You no longer have to draft an email or pick up the phone to reach out to someone else. An important role played by the manager is in the disbursement of information. As a manager, you play the vital link between the higher-ups and employees. Therefore, you must be mindful of social media workgroups.

By leveraging the power of social media workgroups, you can establish an internal communication forum. Internal communication platforms help with quicker decision-making, easier collaboration on different platforms, better employee recognition, and easy communication. When the information travels quickly, it becomes easier to get the required feedback to decide without waiting for the next meeting. Quicker decisions directly influence the profitability of an organisation. The simplest way to get all the employees involved in organisational processes and with each other is through social media. Whether or not they are present at work, employees can stay in touch with one another through these groups. Disbursement of information on social media workgroups is quicker than any of the conventional means. Offering feedback after reviewing a project, updates about the quality of work, and rewards can be facilitated easily through these channels. When you put all these factors together, it increases employee recognition.

A useful tip you need to remember while regulating communication over social media workgroups is establishing ground rules about the content, including what can and cannot be posted. Any information posted on the Internet will stay in the online space forever. So, showing a little vigilance is essential.

Honest Communication

The fear of retribution often prevents employees from expressing their reluctance or disagreeing with the higher-ups within the organisational hierarchy. The simplest way to rectify this is by creating channels for open and honest communication. This is a corporate value that all managers need to incorporate into their management style actively. If the employees are always worried about stepping on toes while voicing their concerns, disagreements, worries, or ideas, it creates a hostile work environment. Making room for open communication ensures employees can open up and speak freely while communicating with their managers.

There are different reasons employees hesitate to open up and communicate freely with their managers. Perhaps they believe the managers will not listen, respond, or even take any action based on employees' input. Or maybe the past managers did not even bother to have opinions. There will be instances when managers use a confrontational approach; condescendingly discount their concerns, issues, and ideas. Whatever is the reason, the lack of open dialogue creates a wide gap between employees and managers within the organisation.

As a manager, it is your responsibility to ensure that there is open communication. To do this, you need to be aware of the organisational core values, communicate about them with employees effectively, and ensure the employees can speak freely.

Here are some tips you can use to achieve this objective.

Acknowledgement

If you want your employees to open up, you need to change your perspective about managing them. Keep an open mind and admit that every individual is unique, and therefore, everyone has a varying viewpoint. By merely showing this acknowledgement, you convey a message that you value what your employees have to share. By spending a little time and energy to get observations, thoughts, and feedback from your employees.

Seek Input

One common mistake managers unknowingly make they brush

away employee input or feedback by saying they don't have the time for it. All managers must take some time to ask that team or employees for suggestions. It is quite simple, but this is one obvious point many managers overlook. Unambiguously communicating that the management is interested in listening to the employees creates a positive work environment.

It is important to seek input or feedback from your employees, but you should ensure that you acknowledge the same. You don't have to act on every information you receive from them, but showing that you were listening and their ideas were considered can work wonders. Doing this shows that their feedback was valued, and they are valuable members of the organisation.

Reflective Listening

All managers need to seek feedback from their employees and communicate that they have heard the opinions and comments they received. The simplest way to do this is by pausing before you reply. You can repeat what the employee said instead of harping on about your opinions. By asking reflective questions or repeating what the employee said, it shows you were listening and interested in understanding what they are saying. When the employees feel heard, their desire to open up and communicate openly increases. While listening, pay attention to the employee's body language, too. The tone, facial expressions, gestures, and general body language can help you understand the emotions behind what they're saying. While doing this, do not invalidate them but give them a chance for open expression.

Personal Engagement

By engaging with your employees regularly, you create a better rapport with them. Something as simple as greeting them or asking them how things are going can create a more relaxed environment at work. As a manager, you are in a position of authority. That said, it doesn't mean you must not be friendly toward employees. A little friendly gesture goes a long way toward ensuring open communication within the organisation and the team. Spend some time and make an effort to understand the role your employees play beyond their professional ones. Showing a slight interest in their lives increases team engagement.

Always Be Respectful

If any of your team members or employees come with suggestions, ideas, or problems, ensure that they have your complete and undivided attention. Whatever you are doing, take a break from it and maintain some eye contact while actively listening. If you don't acknowledge their presence, they will feel unvalued, and it hurts their morale. Don't give your employees the impression that they or whatever they are saying is not essential.

Always Stick To The Schedule

If you have created a plan of action or a timetable, ensure that you follow it. If you continuously reschedule meetings, tell your employees you don't have the time, or cannot show up on time, it reflects poorly on your managerial abilities. Whether it is a staff meeting or a monthly review, stick to the schedule. While creating a timetable, ensure that it is realistic and can be followed. When you are punctual, you are setting a good example for your team members to follow. Apart from that, it also shows your reliability and trustworthiness.

Avoid Judging

If an employee's behaviour, performance, or a decision they made was undesirable, have a personal conversation with them. Instead of publicly chiding, ridiculing, humiliating, or shaming the employee for the things mentioned above, talk to them personally. Instead of judging their behaviour or decisions, describe what you observed. If you noticed that one of your employees frequently misses deadlines, instead of criticising them and calling them a procrastinator, describe what you observed. If you call your employee lazy, it creates discord. If you merely state the delay you observed, you can ask them for the reasons for the same. This can make the employee more forthcoming.

Never Shy Away From Problems

Never shy away from problems, confrontations, or unpleasant conversations. There is always a better way to deal with all these situations, but ignoring or behaving as if they don't exist is undesirable. Whenever you notice a problem, try to fix it immediately. If you ignore or avoid it, the problem festers. It is okay to accept any hurdles or challenges you might face in the workplace.

This helps create a more open environment. When the team knows what is going on and they're not kept in the dark, their willingness to share increases.

Encouraging open and honest communication within an organisation takes conscious effort, time, and energy. All the resources you dedicate toward it will genuinely be worth the results you get.

No Secrets At Work

The need for transparency within an organisation can never be overlooked by creating a company culture based on openness, productivity, and trust.

In the section, let's look at simple steps that all my nails can use to create a transparent one month at work.

Trust Employees

It was repeatedly mentioned that trust is a two-way street. If you want to be trusted, you need to show some trust too. Ensuring a free and honest flow of information within the workspace makes it easier to trust your employees. Have a confidence in your team members to make decisions once you've given them all the information they need. Make it a point that there are no secrets, and all high-level priorities are immediately communicated to all the interested parties.

No Secrecy About Responsibilities And Job Functions

It can be pretty frustrating if most of the time is spent trying to understand who handles what and the person you need to approach in a specific situation. A common mistake a new manager makes is that they don't openly talk about job responsibilities and functions. Even if your idea is not to keep these things secretive, they automatically seem like secrets if you don't talk about them. Instead of wasting your time doing all these things, create a simple list of responsibilities and the corresponding employees responsible for them. This becomes relatively easy to point to ownership and increase awareness of duties within the organisation. And the employees can see who is and isn't responsible for a specific task; their understanding of organisational roles and functions also increases. It may even help you as a new manager to ask staff members to give you a job description as often job responsibilities change over time, and this will also tell you a lot about your employees.

Always Share The Results

Most managers talk much about the next big idea, implementing different policies and seeking feedback from their employees. What good will all this be if there are no results achieved? This is the reason you need to share all the results with your employees. Whether they are good or bad, share or communicate these results. Once you do this, you can look for better alternatives to avoid any mistakes or celebrate outstanding performance.

Allowing the employees to understand what did and did not work allow them to become more efficient. Also, you might never know when someone might come up with better solutions to increase overall efficiency. Whether good or bad, by sharing results, you are increasing the employees' trust in you.

Always Draw The Line

It is important to be transparent, but it is equally important to understand that everything doesn't have to be shared with your employees. Every decision you make doesn't have to be revealed. As long as there is sufficient transparency, it will do. For instance, sharing employees' performance reviews, salary packages, or other sensitive matters doesn't serve any purpose. As long as the information at hand does not violate someone else's right to privacy or a personal matter, it is always better to keep it private.

Create A Safe Space

Remember, no one will want to share unless they feel safe enough to share. By creating a secure workspace that encourages transparency while reducing secrecy, employees' overall productivity will increase. If these employees know they can talk about whatever they feel without rebuke worries, their willingness to share will increase. Create a couple of ground rules about what is and what is not desirable within a team and the organisation. Ensure these rules are in sync with the company objectives. For instance, rules about political correctness and communication can be a good starting point.

Be Mindful Of Political Correctness

The term political correctness has become a part of the regular vocabulary, and it is a moniker. Do you know what political correctness means? Political correctness is a general agreement with the idea that people need to be careful not to behave or use language in a way that can be considered offensive to others. It's so much more than just watching what you say. Political correctness is a broader concept and includes understanding and respecting the differences between individuals that make us unique. It can be challenging and even tricky to determine what to say, how to act, or how to behave after certain cultural or political events, including news about equality, justice, and racism.

Making politically incorrect statements can offend certain groups and land you in hot water. It's not just managers who need to ensure they do not act politically incorrectly, but this is a practice that needs to be followed throughout the organisation.

In this section, let's look at some helpful tips you can use to ensure political correctness.

Start With A Self-Assessment

Political incorrectness often states from conscious or subconscious biases, prejudices, stereotypes, and negative feelings towards a specific individual or even group. To avoid making any politically incorrect statements, it is time for a little self-evaluation. Once you know the emotions or thoughts mentioned above, it becomes easier to change your attitude and behaviour. Admitting biases and prejudices help replace them with desirable ones.

Explore The Information Available

Once you are aware of your prejudices, it's time for a bit of research. Check the other biases, stereotypes, and negative feelings that keep popping up in current events. Notice all these topics and issues that a specific individual or group can consider offensive. While exploring the information available about the subject, chances are it might help invalidate any of your pre-existing biases. Educating yourself is the best way to overcome any preconceptions or prejudices.

Keep Practicing

Now that you have all the information you need and are aware of your biases, it's time to take action to change them. You need to put all your hard work into practice now. Making or breaking a habit takes at least three weeks. During this period, you need to be conscious and mindful of your actions and the statements you make. Avoid politically incorrect thoughts, language, and behaviour. Avoid using gender-specific language or anything that can be construed as exclusionary. Stay away from religious topics and political opinions. Apart from this, be mindful of language and behaviour that can be considered devaluing for those with physical or mental disabilities.

Become Mindful

A golden rule you might have heard is, "Do unto others as you would have them do unto you." Forget about this rule when it comes to staying politically correct. For instance, what might not be offensive to you can be offensive to others. Therefore, before you talk about the previous step's topics, become conscious of what you want to say or your actions. Think about it from someone else's perspective. Also, be mindful of everything you say and do because all this information can be repeated elsewhere.

Being politically correct in the workplace takes conscious effort. It might not seem like it is worth the effort, but it helps establish trust and respect between team members. Following these four simple tips discussed in the section, you can ensure that you avoid making any engaging statements in behaviour deemed politically incorrect.

Tips For Effective Communication

Until now, it was mentioned that managers are responsible for establishing a positive work environment. The simplest way to do this is through effective communication. In this section, let's look at some practical tips you can use to achieve good communication with your team or employees.

Whenever you are communicating, there needs to be clarity. Before you say something, ensure that you think it through. Pay attention to the tips discussed in the previous section about political correctness. Start organising your thoughts, choose words best suited for expressing what you want to say, and convey them understandably. Regardless of the importance of the information you wish to communicate, if you convey it in a language the listener doesn't understand, it is pointless. Also, the words you use need to be adjusted according to the group you are addressing.

Effective communicators are not only willing to express their feelings, but do so efficiently. It doesn't mean they are devoid of emotions. Instead, learn to express your feelings responsibly and professionally. Expressing one's emotions has a human feeling to it. Also, by doing this, you are setting an excellent example for your team and employees. Expression of emotions is essential to build and strengthen the bond with your team.

Communication is so much more than exchanging information or data. This is a part of communication, but it is also an expression of who you are and your feelings. By expressing clear intent, it becomes easier for others to understand where you are coming from.

Learn to be a good listener whenever someone is talking. The first step toward doing this is to be truly present in the conversation. If you are preoccupied with other thoughts, it's doubtful you will pay any attention to what is being said. It also reduces your ability to understand the message that was conveyed. Apart from this, it gives a poor impression that what the other person is saying doesn't matter or is not important. Even if you only have ten minutes, ensure that you give your undivided attention to the employee or team member during this period. After all, you want them to listen to you! If you cannot listen to what they have to say, why would they want to reciprocate?

To become a better listener, ask the right questions, listen actively, and paraphrase the key points the other person conveys. Listen to understand what the other person is saying and where they come from. Instead of merely responding or listening only because you want to answer, listen to understand. While doing this, try to decide on the other person's body language. These skills will come in handy in all your relationships, too.

Effective communicators have empathy. Empathy is the ability to understand what the other person is saying, feeling, and the reasons for the same. You are essentially placing yourself in someone else's shoes to see it from their perspective. Most of us are set in our ways and often struggle to view things from others' point of view. Avoid doing this if you want to become an effective communicator. Showing a little empathy is suitable for any relationship. Empathy helps understand the other person's attitude, thoughts, and feelings. By considering these things, you can become better at communicating the message you want to.

An important skill to communicate effectively is evaluation. Whenever you're listening to someone, regulate your impulses, and resist the urge to respond immediately. By postponing assessment for a while longer, you have time to think things through clearly. Don't be too quick to conclude as soon as an idea is presented. Instead, take time to evaluate and consider it. Resist the urge to judge whether something said is good or bad before you have fully understood it. The lack of this behaviour prevents effective communication and reduces the employees' urge to open up and talk honestly. Also, you might end up missing out on promising ideas because of the inability to evaluate slowly. This is one skill that comes in handy in all aspects of your life, and the sooner you learn, the better it is.

It was mentioned earlier that you need to be empathetic about listening. An important aspect of empathy is to understand different points of view. No two individuals are alike, and therefore, most of us have varying viewpoints about a topic. It is natural, and the sooner you accept it, the better it is. Whenever someone's opinion differs from your own, don't become hostile. Depending on how you deal with opposing views, employees' willingness to communicate freely with you will vary. If you become distressed, feel threatened, or become hostile, chances are the employees will not want to contradict you. It can also become challenging to implement changes when you are unable to understand someone else's perspective. If you want others to consider your perception and attitude, you need to reciprocate. Try to understand what the other person means, the reasons they feel it, and why they support a specific view.

Don't be too fixated on your version of the truth. If additional facts are uncovered, show a willingness to change your convictions and perceptions. Let go of the notion that you always know best or that it is your way or the highway. Just because your ideas or opinions are good doesn't mean others are wrong. Let go of black and white thinking. Learning to keep an open mind is crucial for all managers. It doesn't mean you need to agree with everything others say.

Instead, it means you will listen and change if required. Since change is a constant aspect of life, the sooner you learn to deal with it, the better it is for you.

Conflict resolution and dealing with confrontations are inseparable parts of a manager's responsibilities. Conflict is inevitable. If you want everyone in your team or the employees to express their feelings and thoughts authentically, be prepared for conflicting views and opinions. Unless you learn to deal with these conflicts, it can fester into a significant problem. Confrontations and conflicts are seldom pleasant conversations. With a little tact, professionalism, and empathy, you can make these conversations bearable. You can also ensure that the discussions come to a logical conclusion. Keep your emotions and check, maintain your calm, and use your active listening skills to resolve conflicts. You are in a position of authority, and therefore, you need to face confrontations. While doing this, do so respectfully and assertively.

Another important thing you need to remember regarding conflict resolution is promoting win-win thinking. Instead of believing there will always be winners and losers in every situation, they adopt a win-win approach. Don't get stuck in a win-lose mentality. When it comes to confrontations, ask yourself whether the objectives of both parties involved can be attained. If yes, create a plan of action to achieve it. You will learn more about conflict resolution in the upcoming chapters.

CHAPTER 4: YOU ARE THE COACH, MOTIVATOR, MENTOR, AND TRAINER

As a manager, you play the role of a coach, motivator, mentor, and trainer for everyone you supervise. These are the different roles you need to play simultaneously. Depending on the circumstances, you need to shift from one role to another. In the previous chapter, I introduced you to all the different roles played by a manager. You not only are professionally obligated to play these roles efficiently, but you need to do this to make the most of your team's capabilities. In this chapter, let's learn more about how you can efficiently and effectively play each role.

Training Team Members

Many new managers are surprised when they realise they need to train their employees and team members. Regardless of how big or small your team or department is, you need to manage them. To improve supervisory success, you need to train them. This section looks at practical tips you can use to promote employee development and training.

Before you start training, you need to realise your training responsibilities. All the employees need to be adequately prepared to ensure they carry out their responsibilities and duties properly. Whether the organisation has a specific or dedicated training department or not, every manager needs to train their team. You need to prepare each of your team members and subordinates to optimise team success.

Now that you have understood, your team needs the training to concentrate on what they need to know. Offering training, which applies to the tasks they complete or their designated roles, proves fruitful. Likewise, if you provide training opportunities that are irrelevant to their organisational roles and responsibilities, the motivation to undergo such training decreases. Make a note of the unique skills required to perform the tasks and duties efficiently and effectively. Apart from that, don't forget to train them in organisational policies, teamwork, procedures, and desirable behaviours.

Learning to train efficiently is as important as determining the training your team needs. Understand the difference between training your employees and telling them what they need to do. While training, you need to convey instructions and information efficiently, resulting in skill transfer. Even if you're not the one undertaking the training program, you need to ensure it is the right one for your employees. Depending on their personalities and learning styles, the training program needs to change. Some learn better through hands-on experience, while others require plenty of reading matter. By spending a little time and getting to know your team on a personal level, it becomes easier to devise a tailor-made training program.

Regardless of how efficient your training program is or how fantastic your ideas are, it doesn't lead to success if your employees are not on board with that training. The best way to do this is by explaining what they stand to gain. By conveying the relevance of the employee training, you increase their inherent motivation to work better. It's not just important to stress the organisational benefits, but personal benefits too.

After your team members or employees have undergone the specific training, ensure that you verify their grasp of the skills learned. There is no point in training them if you don't check what they have learned. By seeking feedback and observing their performance, you can ensure they have gained the new skills or abilities you want. Also, training is not a one-time process. It is a job that needs to be undertaken regularly. Since organisations do not exist in a vacuum, and the environment is dynamic, they need to keep up with all these changes. Therefore, work on training your employees regularly. To optimise the success of employee training, don't forget to seek feedback from them. After all, they are the ones who are directly affected by it, and by understanding what they truly need, you can create better training programs in the future.

Motivation Matters

One of the crucial aspects that determines a department's performance and even the organisation is employee motivation. Motivating your team and employees is an integral part of your managerial position. Employees motivation depends on all the interactions they have with their managers. When the employees are better motivated, it ensures the company's objectives are met. It increases the productivity of different employees while allowing the organisation to improve its overall results. If the employees are not motivated to work but wiles away their time, it wastes precious resources. Without motivation, it becomes tough to achieve the desired goals. The thing with motivation is that it is an internal factor.

Highly motivated employees are more committed to their work. Motivated employees continuously work on developing and improving themselves and are satisfied. When employees are satisfied, it ensures the company, or the organisation, is growing in the right direction. Motivation helps employees achieve their personal goals and increases the scope for self-development. Once they attain some initial plans, they will realise the direct relationship between their efforts and the results. This will entice them to do even better. When you put all these factors together, you realise that motivation increases employee efficiency.

Now that you realise the importance of inspiring your employees, here are some tips you can use to enhance their motivation immediately.

Better Communication

The simplest way to enhance employee motivation at work is through positive communication. In the previous section, you were introduced to different tips and techniques you can follow to become an efficient communicator. By being an excellent role model, you are encouraging your employees to follow suit. It's not just about communication via emails and other electronic media. Make sure that you talk to them in person, too. We can never underestimate the power of personal meetings and conversations. Take some time daily and converse with your employees. By doing this, you are making them feel like they are a valuable part of the team. Simultaneously, it also helps the employees understand you are a part of the team and are not just their boss. Team communication is critical to improving employee motivation and attitude.

Recognise Individual Contributions

All managers must ensure that their teams know the importance of their contributions. By understanding the roles they play in the achievement of organisational objectives, they will feel more valued. When the employees know their contributions matter, they take pride in their work. This will increase their engagement at work and make them more motivated. When they know their efforts don't go to waste and create an impact within the organisation, regardless of how big or small they are, they will feel better. The rewards don't have to be anything significant. Acknowledging the effort they make will be sufficient.

Create A Positive Environment

Never underestimate the importance of a positive workplace environment. If an unhealthy competition or the workplace environment is toxic, it harms employees' motivation levels. The simplest way to rectify this situation is by conducting surveys and getting feedback from the employees. In the previous chapter, you were introduced to different tips you can use as a manager to get a better understanding of the organisational culture. By creating a positive corporate culture, you are directly improving the motivation levels of different employees.

Team Development

Even experienced managers require reminders to understand they are sitting on a goldmine of potential. What is this potential? It essentially refers to latent employee talents. Don't get so caught up in the regular activities that you forget about team development. If you don't enhance your team's skills and capabilities, you cannot expect enhanced productivity. If the team members are stuck in an uninspiring role, their motivation to do better will reduce.

A manager's responsibility is to gather the required information about the employees' skills and developmental needs. By understanding their career goals and assessing their existing skill sets, you can offer developmental opportunities. When the employees realise that management is involved and interested in their personal and professional development, they become more motivated to do better.

In this section, let's look at helpful tips you can use to promote team development.

Start Talking

If you want to know what your employees want, there is only one thing you need to do! Talk to them. Seek information about their personal and professional goals. Ask them how they can attain these goals and the future they desire. The continued success and progress of an organisation depends on the talent of its employees. Even though most managers realise the importance of training for creating a high-performing team, they don't take the time required to understand their team members' specific needs or goals. By determining their needs, motivation, and goals, you get a better sense of what they need to become better at their responsibilities. Individual training requirements might be universal, while others depend on the personal capabilities of employees.

Once the employee has undergone the organisation's orientation program and has a thorough understanding of the job requirements, the employee development methods need to be unique; every person has a different responsibility and role. Their objectives, levels of knowledge, personal capabilities, and skills differ. Therefore, managers need to provide the proper training to the right employees at the right time.

By asking the questions mentioned above, you get a better understanding of their perspective. For instance, by asking your employees about the unique challenges they face daily or the aspects of their job that frustrate them, you have more information to create desirable suggestions and solutions to maximise their effectiveness.

Synchronisation Between Developmental Efforts And Expectations

Every role has a specific job description. Spend some time and review all the job descriptions and list the core competencies required for each of these roles. Once you've completed this groundwork, brainstorm with others to determine the projects or training activities that will help your employees develop the skills associated with each of their positions. You can also use the job description or the competency model provided by your organisation to make better decisions. The scope and complexity of the developmental tasks and responsibilities you give your team will be based on your review of the aforementioned information. You will learn more about job descriptions in the subsequent chapters.

Remember, the organisation's competency model or the job description may not be ideal for all employees. Instead, evaluate your team members and identify the gaps between their existing skills and those they need to work on. By bridging this gap, it becomes easier to offer them the required opportunities to grow and develop. Another simple technique you can use here is to discuss potential options and improvement areas with the concerned team members. While doing this, use a non-threatening approach. Instead of positioning yourself as an adversary, approach it from a problem-solution perspective and work together with the team member.

The developmental framework of core competencies that exist in organisations is usually generic. They serve as a skeletal structure that can be fleshed out depending on the needs and interests of different individuals. As a manager, you need to understand the framework and create a plan of action to help your team members develop and grow.

Professional Development And Work Culture

Professional development is not restricted to developing the required job skills. It is so much more than that. It is about finding new ways to improve intellectual talent, creative potential, and untapped energy to increase talent collection within an organisation. Professional development needs to become a part of the regular work culture in an organisation. When employees within an organisation know that the management is invested in their professional development, they will be more engaged. It also sets the tone for what they can expect from the company. After all, the relationship between an organisation and its employees is not one-sided. If the business needs to grow, the employees need to succeed.

Show Your Commitment And Support

The importance of showing how much you care for and value your team members cannot be overstated. You need to show that you genuinely care about them as individuals and not just employees. By showing that you are focused on their growth and development, you can create an invested team. If you expect personal investment and engagement from your team, be willing to reciprocate. Don't treat your team and employees like cogs in a machine.

Whenever you create any developmental plans for your employees' benefit, ensure that you consider their feedback and input. Doing this helps increase their loyalty and strengthens their commitment while earning their respect. If you treat them as expendable resources, you cannot hold on to them for long. Therefore, become a leader who listens to their followers.

Truly listen and pay attention to what the employees want and communicate. Consider their opinions while helping their development. When you share responsibility with the employees, they become more invested in their tasks. For instance, it is a waste of time and resources to drag unwilling employees toward training programs they are not interested in. By sharing responsibilities, you reduce the risk of this happening. Professional development is not a one-time event, and it certainly isn't a standalone process. The managers and employees need to be equally involved in this process.

Help Your Team Grow

In the previous section, you were introduced to tips to help team and employee development. Helping your team grow is a crucial aspect of any managerial job. Here are some suggestions you can use to help your team succeed.

By encouraging the professional development of the employees, you are helping them grow. Remember, all employees dream of climbing the corporate ladder. If the existing status quo is unsatisfactory to employees, especially those with high potential, they will become discontent. Offer proper guidance and help them achieve different levels of professional development. By helping your team grow, you are enhancing the overall output of your team and their efficiency.

You can facilitate employee growth by establishing skills in sync with their interests, professional experience, and personal strengths. By doing this, you can ensure their personal goals are in synchronisation with the business strategy and objectives. Through establishing reasonable goals, you are also effectively communicating your expectations.

You can create an internal mentorship program if you find others who are similar to the employee. Mentoring helps foster positive and productive relationships that develop employee engagement. When each employee is invested in their growth and others, team bonding and cohesiveness increase; it also helps establish positive team dynamics that are crucial for team success.

Another simple technique you can use for employee development is to help them establish their personal networks. Show them various opportunities that exist within the organisation while encouraging them to network with other professional groups. By building professional contacts and connections, you increase their potential.

The simplest way to encourage employee development is by giving them challenging assignments. If they are continually working within their comfort zones, the scope for development of growth is minimum. By giving them challenging tasks, you are helping improve their professional skills. It also allows them to take stock of their existing skills and capabilities. It may also help you discover their hidden talents or potential.

If you are genuinely invested in the development of your team and employees, show your trust. Trust that they will get the job done and will do it well. Before you do this, ensure that you communicate your expectations. You can also model the behaviour and attitude you expect. Apart from this, you also need to show that you trust them. Your show of trust shows the employees they have what it takes to succeed and increases their ownership.

Learn To Get Involved

If you want to increase your team's productivity and success, you need to engage the employees. An organisation benefits from this level of understanding of its workforce's passion for the job. As a manager, the responsibility lies on your shoulders to ensure that your team members take pride in what they do and their work.

Individuals who have a sense of purpose and understand their value put their best foot forward. This is a practice that will benefit the entire organisation. Spend some time understanding the work people do, why they do it, and their motivating factors.

Since you are in a managerial role, understanding your employees is a crucial part of the successful evaluation of staff engagement. From their skills to personal life and hobbies, various aspects of an employees life become vital in the overall workplace and management. Once you are armed with this knowledge, you can use it to create a productive and positive environment.

So, what does employee engagement mean? It's not just about the knowledge of whether someone likes or dislikes the job. It shows how committed an employee is to the business and its success. It shows their motivations and personal investment in the work. An engaged employee is better motivated to put in the required effort toward a company's common goals while working on personal development. They are committed to the core values represented by the organisation. They also clearly understand the company objectives and the importance of the work they do.

With employee engagement, there are two primary aspects you need to concentrate on. You need to understand the level of engagement within the organisation, and the second aspect is to understand the level of engagement with managers. By looking at the relationship between managers and employees, you know how the employees feel about their direct supervisors.

If an employee has higher engagement levels with their manager, it means they're working in the right direction and are happy with the work. It represents mutual respect between employees and managers. When the employee engagement levels are relatively high within an organisation, it shows the workforce or employees trust their leader.

In this section, let's look at some simple techniques you can use to increase employee engagement.

Personal Meetings

The simplest way to understand your employees, their motivations, and desires is by scheduling personal meetings with them. Instead of team gatherings, conduct one-on-one meetings with them. Get to know your new team members, their strengths, goals, priorities, and weaknesses. These frequent meetings show you care and are invested in their development. Apart from this, you also get an opportunity to communicate about any likely changes that will increase the team's efficiency while working on shared goals and objectives.

Giving And Receiving Feedback

Feedback is essential because it helps employees understand what they are expected to do, whether they are doing it well, and the areas they need to improve. This might seem like an intimidating process to your employees, but it is a vital part of your job description. By understanding and listening to the comments you receive from your team members, you can reduce tension and improve their productivity. Depending on the employees' needs and preferences, personalise how the assessment is delivered. During these conversations, pay attention to how specific employees like to receive feedback. Change your managerial style based on circumstances and the employee you are dealing with.

While offering your observations, ensure that each of your employees knows you have their best interest in mind. This will make them more open to the feedback they receive while encouraging them to share their comments. By allowing them to offer an honest opinion about your performance, you can ensure you are working together as a team. After all, your team's performance is influenced by your managerial style. By receiving feedback about yourself, you can change your executive style according to your team's needs.

The need for open and honest communication and a transparent workplace has been stressed repeatedly throughout chapters of this book. Open communication is vital to fuel collaboration and new ideas. Without open and honest communication, none of this can be achieved. If the employees feel they have no voice in the organisation, it will create dissatisfaction. This discontent can reduce their overall efficiency and effectiveness. You are a leader for your team members and an advocate for their growth and development.

Obstacles And Solutions

Most new managers feel demotivated and discouraged whenever they face obstacles or complications. If you want to feel more comfortable in your new role, you must acknowledge the problems that crop up. Once you are aware of the issues or obstacles, work together with your team to come up with helpful solutions. If you don't want to get blindsided by significant problems in the future, confront any hurdles in their nascent stage. It is easier to nip a problem in the bud. If needed, seek your team member's guidance or support to solve a problem. After all, you are a team, and you need to work together.

Instruct And Explain

An efficient manager provides direction and plays the role of a teacher to his employees and the members. You need to be good at instructing and explaining to achieve this aim. Here are some simple steps you can use in this process.

Before you expect your team or employees to complete a task you assigned, ensure that you offer some context. When others understand the importance of the job, they need to complete and their role in an organisation, the willingness to work increases; you convey a positive message of respect when you take the time to discuss and explain the importance of the task that needs to be completed. While assigning duties, roles, and responsibilities, ensure that you are incredibly specific. Your instructions will yield nothing significant if the tasks you have set are vague. By giving a basic outline, it becomes easier to determine specific quality standards.

Whenever you are instructing or explaining anything to your team or employees, always be respectful. Do not compromise here. Regardless of how stressful the circumstances are, don't forget to be respectful. While giving instructions, give your team a chance to ask questions too. By doing this, you are strengthening the communication between employees and their supervisors. It also increases the chances of better outcomes. When the employees know they are valued and are free to ask whatever they want, their willingness to do better will improve.

Work on reinforcing your team's confidence by offering positive feedback whenever appropriate. If you believe there is a scope for improvement or witness undesirable behaviour, provide constructive feedback. Apart from this, trust your team and employees to do well without giving in to the urge to micromanage.

A manager's vital role is to assess if any further training is required for the team members or employees. If you realise there is some scope for learning, step into the teacher's role, and explain the concept to your team members. If you believe training is required, get on it immediately and offer them the training they need. By providing instruction and learning opportunities, you are creating a positive work culture.

Whenever you explain anything to your team or employees, ensure that you view it from their perceptive. Listen actively and respond to questions they ask. Avoid interrupting others and stay present in the conversation. If you use any acronyms or words, others might not know, take a pause and explain it. Do not talk down to your team and employees. Apart from this, ask them questions to determine their level of understanding. If you believe your team hasn't understood it well enough, start this process again. Make analogies and provide examples to enhance your team's understanding of a specific concept. If you believe there are certain similarities between the ideas, they already know and the new ones you are teaching, then draw parallels. It is always easier to build upon something the employees already know, so you need to draw on it.

While instructing or explaining anything to your team and employees, ensure that you ask them if they have understood what you're conveying. Creating a positive work environment and an open culture makes it easier for others to ask questions. Do not be impatient while answering and make sure that they've all fully understood everything you are trying to convey.

Delegate And Support

Delegation is an essential aspect of a manager's daily duties. It might not be an easy responsibility, especially for new managers, but it is vital for your growth and your team's development. Most managers stay comfortable making the same decisions they've always made. This stems from the belief that they know and can always do better than others. To avoid losing control of a situation or specific result, they don't give authority or responsibilities to their subordinates. The action or process of assigning authority to another person for carrying out a particular function or duty is known as delegation. It is essentially the distribution of power. Delegation is also a show of confidence, trust, and faith that a manager has in the team's abilities.

Managers need to entrust responsibilities and offer support. You need to let go of the need for control and play a supporting role. Remember, managers have the responsibility of developing individual team members. If you do not offer them an opportunity for personal growth and development, it creates employee dissatisfaction. To avoid all this, here are some things you can follow while delegating responsibilities and supporting your team members.

Tips To Delegate Responsibilities

When it comes to sharing your responsibilities, the earlier you start, the better. Delegating tasks early reduces unnecessary pressure and allows the other individual to create a better plan to achieve the desired results or goals. Before you delegate a responsibility, ensure that you are entrusting it to the right person. Assess the capabilities and skills of your employees before assigning them a task. For instance, giving the responsibility of creating a sales plan to someone in the product research department doesn't make much sense.

While delegating responsibilities, ensure that you communicate the employee's benefits by completing the task. Apart from this, talk about how and why a specific task was entrusted to a particular individual. When you delegate, ensure that a specific responsibility is given to a single person. If you trust the same job to multiple people, it creates chaos and ambiguity.

An essential rule, while the delegation of responsibilities, is to establish clear goals and expectations. When employees know what they need to do and what is expected of them, they get a better sense of their goals and responsibilities; by offering information about what, why, when, who and where, you are increasing the employee's efficiency.

Your job doesn't end after delegating a task. You should also trust the required authority and responsibility to ensure the assigned task is completed efficiently. Allow your team member or employee to complete the job as they see fit. You can offer feedback and support when required, but learn to take a step back. Be willing to keep an open mind and accept any suggestions made by the employee.

You need to take a personal interest in the employee's progress while working on a delegated task. From offering support and instructions to guidance, these simple activities show your involvement and engagement. While doing all this, remember not to micromanage. If your delegating style becomes too intrusive, it can cause feelings of frustration and resentment within the employee.

While delegating a responsibility, chances are there will be instances when you are not fully satisfied with the employee's progress. In such cases, don't immediately withdraw the project or reassign it to someone else. Instead, take the time to offer advice about the changes that can be made. This ensures employee dependability and accountability. If you are delegating responsibility to someone who has no previous experience, ensure you offer the guidance and help.

Once the task is completed, don't forget to offer feedback. Spend time to evaluate and recognise the performance of the employee. By providing feedback, you are effectively helping the employee make the required changes to generate better results in the future.

Tips To Support Your Team

Supporting your team is a crucial role played by every manager. You should not only help them during a crisis, but do it daily. Instead of waiting for a quarterly review, check-in with your team daily and have weekly meetings. By regularly checking the progress and offering them assistance as and when required, it shows your support. Another gesture of providing complete support to your team is by sticking up for them. There will be instances when others in the organisation will criticize your team. It can be relatively easy to take all the credit for the good they do while shying away from responsibility when things don't go right. Avoid doing this and, instead, stick up for your team. If you know your team did everything they could, they must understand you will stick up for them. The simple act of standing up for them creates better trust and bonding.

Whenever you have delegated any accountability to someone on the team, communicate about it early. It's not just the individual who needs to know, but the entire team does, too. This ensures that no one is caught off guard, and they know their specific roles and responsibilities.

By setting specific standards, you can ensure that your team is producing the best results. Setting standards offers a sense of direction and creates a benchmark. This also provides some consistency in how the group operates. By helping your team members improve their professional skills, you are supporting them. Offer them sufficient opportunities to develop their skills. This will improve confidence that increase their motivation to do better.

Motivate And Inspire

Here are some tips you can use to motivate and inspire your team to do better.

Set Goals

The primary source of internal motivation is the process of setting goals and achieving them. When you are interested in something, your motivation to accomplish it is higher. This is a reason you need to set individual goals for your team members. These targets need to be clear, measurable, relevant, and time-bound. When you set reasonable goals, it reduces misunderstandings while telling the employees what is expected of them. Plans also help measure the progress they make while showing any areas of improvement.

Empower Your Team

By getting your team members directly involved in the decision-making process, you empower them: your employees' responsibility and ownership increase when they become a part of the decision-making process. Whenever there are any problems or obstacles, the team faces, ensure you facilitate group discussions about them and offer support when required. Always encourage and motivate them to solve these problems on their own. The best thing you can do is sit back and let your team do the work. Trust their ability to solve the problem instead of swooping in and offering a solution immediately. Start delegating more responsibilities and tasks to them as their commitment, confidence, and competence increase. Permit your team members to make some decisions. When they have to deal with the consequences of the decisions, it teaches them personal accountability and ownership.

Don't Forget To Offer Support

Since the organisation exists in a dynamic environment, change is a constant factor. Change means the team members frequently need to upgrade their skills and understanding of topics to enhance their work efficiency. As a manager, allow them to develop and try fresh approaches. Be supportive of their ideas and encourage training and developmental programs.

Always Communicate The Vision

Communicating the vision might sound like a simple idea. However, the challenging part of it is to inspire others to follow you and attain the vision. The simplest way to ensure that your team is motivated to work toward your vision is through clear and unambiguous communication. This is one of those things that is easier said than done. Chances are, some might or might not agree with what you want them to do. In such situations, do not impose your vision on them. Instead, try to talk about the benefits it offers. By showing them all that distance to gain by working toward your vision, their motivation to do better will increase. While doing this, don't forget to accept responsibility for your actions. This will be an excellent learning opportunity for all your team members.

Appreciate And Value Your Team

The simplest way to motivate and inspire your team to do better is by investing your time and resources in them. When they see your involvement, they will feel valued and appreciated. Giving them a chance to express themselves openly and with no judgment increases respect in the relationship. When you put all these elements together, it creates a strong bond between the team members and the manager. By recognising their effort, input, and commitment, you are expressing how valuable they are.

Their inherent desire to work better and more efficiently increases when they know they are valued and appreciated. The knowledge that their efforts are recognised increases self-satisfaction. Apart from valuing and appreciating your employees, don't forget to respect them. Everyone likes to be respected. The thing with respect is, it needs to be earned. By setting some ground rules, you can show your employees how they can appreciate them.

Truly Understand Your Employees

If you want to inspire your team and employees, you need to understand them. Without prior knowledge of the individuals who make up your team, you cannot inspire or motivate them. Inspiration and motivation are personal factors. Unless they stem from within, they will not be of much use. Understanding your employees, their tendencies, thought processes, and behaviours make it easier to motivate them.

Do not make the mistake of believing that your title or position in the organisation will inspire them. By taking an interest in them and playing an active part in the team processes, you can boost and motivate them. This is the only way to do it, and there are no shortcuts here.

Growth And Development

If you have your team's best interests at heart, then you will be invested in their growth and development. When the employees can see the steps taken to increase their professional capabilities, their performance will improve. By mentoring and guiding them toward growth and developmental opportunities, you are inspiring them to do better. This also creates a strong sense of belonging and togetherness. When the team members are aligned with the departmental or team goals, they feel more inspired and encouraged to do a better job. Also, such a team willingly accepts responsibility for all their actions.

Mentor And Coach

If you want to help your team improve and develop their skills, you need to have a mentoring and coaching relationship with them. If you are caught up in your work and are spending all your time in meetings, you might not have much time or energy to help your team grow and develop. This section will teach you some practical and straightforward tips you can use to ensure you are mentoring and coaching your team while dealing with your other responsibilities and obligations.

Schedule Check-Ins

Instead of making unscheduled check-ins, schedule regular meetings. Time management is a vital skill, and the sooner you learn it, the better for your development and that of the team. By scheduling regular meetings with each team member, it becomes easier to have meaningful and purposeful interactions. This doesn't mean you don't have any time available for emergencies and important questions. However, train and encourage your team members to distinguish between issues that warrant immediate attention and the ones that can wait for a while. All the non-urgent conversations can be left for a later date. By scheduling a specific slot, it ensures that there is no time wastage.

Once the meeting time arrives, ensure that you spend it wisely. Communicate with your team that the reports they need to present should include all their concerns and questions. Apart from this, encourage them to think about potential solutions before presenting their problems or concerns. By doing this, you not only save sufficient time, but also increase employee participation and engagement. Since you consider your employees' opinions and views, it equips them with better problem-solving skills. If any specific ideas appeal to you, implement them. If you believe there is room for improvement, suggest it.

Problem-Solving Skills

A simple way to empower your team through coaching and mentoring is by encouraging them to solve their problems. If you are continually dealing with simple requests, it is time for you to reconsider your management style. If you keep swooping in or start micromanaging every step your team members take, you are slowly but surely undermining their sense of self-reliance. As a manager, it is your responsibility to offer the tools and training coupled with the autonomy required to solve the problems they face. If you provide them solutions, the minute a problem arises, they will never learn problem-solving skills.

If your team is facing a challenge, encourage them to work through it. You can play an instrumental role by helping them identify the important resources they need to solve the problem or challenge. However, give them the liberty required to implement their solutions. You need to create a team that is self-sufficient and reliant. They need to be able to work independently without your

3333333

constant guidance. Once they become accustomed to the delegation of responsibilities and independence, they will become adept at their jobs.

The Rules About Mentoring And Coaching

Mentoring and coaching are the full-time responsibilities of all managers. You cannot schedule a specific time to mentor or coach employees. Instead, it is an ongoing process. Whenever an opportunity presents itself that you believe can be a teaching moment, communicate with your employees. While coaching or mentoring your employees, ensure that you offer input about areas of improvement. Work together to identify the areas and unique skills they require to improve themselves and further their careers. After this, show them the training resources to get all the information they need to head in the right direction.

Signs Of Burnout And Disengagement

When your team starts underperforming, seems disengaged and quite cynical, the first thing that pops into your mind is probably the lack of discipline. If you notice these signs from a team or an employee who usually performs well, it can be a sign of burnout. If an employee is subjected to excess stress, is overworked, doesn't get challenging assignments, or is tasked with routine work, it can reduce productivity. Regardless of the cause, productivity will decline if the employee is drained out. The most effective means to tackle burnout is by recognising its signs. After all, prevention is better than cure. In this section, let's look at the signs of burnout and disengagement at the workplace and tips to remedy them.

The most common sign of disengagement or burnout is the reduction in overall productivity and work quality. Whether it is an employee or a team, this is the first sign you need to pay attention to. If your team or employee starts missing deadlines, the quality of work has reduced, or is shying away from assuming responsibility; it is time to look at the situation. Don't assume procrastination or laziness as the cause. The issue might be more profound than this. If you notice this irresponsible or lax behaviour from a consistently dependable employee, it can be because of disengagement or burnout.

If a team is excited and happy within the organisation, they are eager to make suggestions, offer feedback, and collaborate on different tasks and challenges. If the team suddenly disconnects or an employee withdraws, it is a sign of burnout. Take corrective measures if you notice any unusual disengagement within the team.

Another sign of burnout and disengagement you need to watch out for is the increase in complaining and cynicism. If a usually optimistic employee mumbles about all the things that can go wrong or seems frustrated for no apparent reason, it is a red flag. If an enthusiastic team becomes quite pessimistic and starts complaining about different activities or tasks, do not ignore it. Occasional complaints and pessimism are common. However, if this becomes a commonplace occurrence, you need to pay attention to it.

Now that you are aware of different signs of burnout and disengagement, you need to take action. If left unchecked, they can fester into a significant problem. If you don't take any corrective action to fix the situation, it can become challenging later.

Here are some tips you can use to rectify employee disengagement and burnout.

Identify The Reason

Unless you identify the reason that caused the team or employees atypical behaviour, it's doubtful you can avoid this in the future. They can be different personal and professional factors that might have caused the unfavourable change in the employee performance or attitude. The simplest way to uncover the truth is by having an honest conversation. It can be a drastic or an unpleasant change in their personal life, such as an illness, death in the family, or anything else that troubles them. Professionally, the person might be dissatisfied with their role in the team or the organisation. When employees get stuck doing the same thing over and over, it tires them and causes disinterest. Another common reason is stress. An honest conversation can help identify the reason and give you better insight into the problem. Once you have the required information, creating a plan of action to rectify the situation becomes more manageable.

The Need For Balance

Suppose one of your employees or team members has way too

many responsibilities and is overworked. In that case, chances are they end up compromising their personal life to make time for their professional responsibilities. Working long hours isn't necessarily a sign of progress or development. For instance, many people wrongly assume that working long hours conveys the message that they are hard workers. It might be true. However, it also results in exhaustion, unhappiness, and frustration. If you notice that one of your employees or team members is disengaged and seems to be burnt out, come up with a successful way to deal with this behaviour. By talking about the need for a balance between professional and personal life, you can reduce the chances of negative attitudes creeping in. Don't forget to have a conversation with your employee about this. Create a tactical plan of action to tackle the situation and reverse the disengagement. By acknowledging your expectations and conveying the same to the employee, you relieve a little of their stress. For instance, don't encourage your team members to work long hours, but establish daily deadlines and timelines. Ensure that they get sufficient breaks during a typical workday. All it takes is a little conscious effort to ensure your team members and employees strike the perfect balance between personal and professional life. Once this balance is present, the disengagement will reduce.

Switch Responsibilities

An effective means to reduce employee disengagement and prevent burnout is by switching things around. Don't make things too routine and change things up from time to time. For instance, if one of your team members is always assigned the most demanding clients, change their responsibilities. Assign these clients to someone else. Even if the other person isn't as experienced as the former, they are learning. Offer them different roles and tasks instead of the same ones. When you perform the same job over and over, it becomes mundane and boring.

By reducing the workload and equally distributing it between various team members, you give them a chance to breathe. Also, vary the type of projects that are assigned to your team members. For instance, if one of your team members crunches numbers and performs financial analysis, give them a creative job or assignment for a while. This ensures they are continually learning new skills required to increase their professional efficiency while creating scope for personal development. By merely changing the day-to-day routine, the team member's excitement and energy for the work will improve.

Apart from all this, all managers need to remember that employee burnout and disengagement will not fix themselves. Instead, as a manager, it is your responsibility to ensure you help your employees get back on the right track. If you step in and offer the required help at the right time, it will create a positive change.

Influence Others

Authority doesn't grant influence. An influential manager knows how to inspire and help others achieve their true potential, exudes confidence, and is trusted and respected by the employees. Do not make the mistake of taking on an aggressive style of management to convey your assertiveness. You can also not be a good mentor or a coach if all you do is inspire fear. Being confident doesn't mean you have to intimidate others. If you take on an aggressive approach, it shows you don't trust your employees to do well.

An important aspect of a manager's job is to influence others. Remember, there's a difference between influence and manipulation. Manipulation is seldom desirable and is a negative tactic regardless of the intention with which it is used. On the other hand, influence essentially suggests the ability to affect someone else's behaviour through a thought process. By influencing your employees, you can motivate them to do better. It also gives you the power required to ensure your team is on board with all the changes that take place. Without some level of influence, you cannot get your team to do your bidding.

This section looks at some suggestions that new managers can use to influence the teams toward success.

Your Personality Matters

Do not become too eager to prove your mettle and make drastic changes without talking about it with your team. Consult the employees before making significant changes in the workplace. If you don't include your employees in this process, it will quickly erode their trust in you and your leadership. It also conveys the wrong message or doesn't value your team members' feedback or opinions enough to consider them. Similarly, if you isolate yourself from your team and other employees, it creates an unnecessary gap. Bridging the divide later will be difficult. A critical task on your list of priorities is to establish strong and healthy relationships with those you supervise as a new manager.

The simplest way to do this is by making yourself seem more relatable. Start sharing your experiences in personal and professional lives where you overcame obstacles, try to create a friendly and welcome atmosphere that puts others at ease, and efficiently communicate about your vision, goals, and how it correlates to their personal development. Apart from this, take some time and truly get to know your team by asking for feedback about what they like, the changes they want to see, and areas where there is scope for improvement. Instead of keeping your employees in the dark, include them in the decision-making process, especially on the decisions which directly affect their work.

Be A Good Role Model

Let go of the "Do as I say, not as I do" mentality. Whenever you are delegating any responsibilities, ensure that you show the team member how it needs to be executed. Doing this reduces the fear of failure on the employees and permits them to make certain mistakes. If you constantly reprimand or penalise employees for their errors, it probably means they were not offered the right tools or guidance at the right time, and it creates a hostile work culture. This can harm the team dynamic and reduce its overall efficiency.

If you want to influence your team members, you must model the behaviour you expect from others. You need to lead by example. If you want your team to be collaborative and respectful, you need to display these traits. If you don't, you set a poor example.

After all, what good reason do they have to follow you if you cannot follow your own advice?

Improve Your Communication Skills

I talk about all the different tips and techniques you can use to enhance your communication skills to become an effective communicator in previous chapters. Communication is a two-way street, and learning to communicate your plans and expectations is essential. Apart from this, you should also receive feedback from your employees about your goals and expectations. When your team members feel included and valued, they are naturally more inclined to listen to you. If you expect your team's compliance, be willing to reciprocate. The simplest way to do this is by enhancing your communication skills. Effective and efficient communication ensures there is no ambiguity, while everyone in the team or the organisation knows their designated roles and responsibilities. Apart from that, they also understand the role they play in the organisation while achieving different objectives.

By encouraging your team members to communicate openly and honestly, you create a positive environment. When your team members trust, respect, and are confident about each other and their capabilities, their willingness to collaborate increases. If your team members trust and respect you and are confident about your skills and abilities, they will be more inclined to listen to you. If you are not an effective communicator, you cannot achieve this goal.

Recognition And Growth Are Crucial

When the employees within a team know the manager is always looking out for them and is concerned about their recognition and growth, it increases their trust in you. Creating a work culture that promotes collaboration and development increases your influence on your team. If the employees can see how much the manager is invested in their development, their motivation to do better and not disappoint them increases. You should concentrate on furthering yourself in the organisation and focus on your employee's growth. This connectedness culture increases employee motivation and gives you a better chance of influencing them in the right direction.

CHAPTER 5: SUCCESS IS DEFINED BY THE TEAM

Building Team Dynamics

Organisational success depends on team dynamics. It becomes easier to leverage employees' full potential and make the most of all the skills and experience when the team dynamics are positive. In this section, let's learn how to build and improve team synergy for better performance.

An interconnected and interdependent relationship between two or more individuals working together to attain a specific goal is known as a team. Teams can be established for achieving short-term and long-term objectives. Group dynamics essentially help understand how a particular member's distinct rules and behaviours influence the entire group. Team dynamics are the psychological and subconscious factors that significantly affect the team's behaviour, performance, and direction.

Positive team dynamics means that the team members trust and work with each other effectively and efficiently. They can make collective decisions and don't mind sharing accountability for the same. The team's entire behaviour with positive team dynamics is more productive and representative of shared mutual understanding and self-corrective actions. When the dynamics are negative, it reduces the overall effectiveness and efficiency of the team. The success rate of the team directly influences the bottom line of an organisation. Building positive team dynamics is the full-time responsibility of a manager.

Here are some tips you can use to achieve this aim.

Understand Your Team

You need to run a check to determine the overall health and wellbeing of your team. Observe how they work and conduct themselves with each other and in personal spaces. Get feedback from other relevant people, including customers, and other team managers, to understand if there is any problem with your team. The common causes of poor team dynamics include excessive deference to authority, free riding, apprehension of employees, and aggressive or hostile behaviours from specific team members. By running a team diagnostic check, you will understand the areas where there is a scope for improvement. Lack of effective communication, overall negative attitude, or any other behaviour that prevents the free flow of information in the group can be reasons for poor team dynamics unless you know why you cannot take action to rectify and change it for the better.

Quickly Resolve Conflicts

If you notice someone in the team is not displaying helpful behaviours or is engaging in unhelpful activities, address the problem quickly. Resolve conflicts immediately. The best way to go about doing this is by having a one-on-one conversation with the concerned team member to discuss their behaviour and offer solutions to change it. As long as there is an open and honest discussion, conflict resolution becomes more effortless.

Draft A Team Charter

Poor team dynamics can also result from a lack of clarity. Creating a team charter makes it easier for team members to understand the specific roles, purposes, responsibilities, and power available. This helps motivate them to do better. It also offers particular benchmarks that can improve the performance of any underperforming members.

Good Communication

Communication is essential in any relationship, whether personal or professional. In a team, building effective lines of communication is critical. Ensure that the team members have the required tools to communicate with each other openly. Set specific ground rules for communication and ensure that the team members are always in the loop about any recent developments, changes, or alterations.

Team Culture Matters

For a team to attain its goal, each member needs to help and support others. By maintaining open and honest lines of communication and encouraging inclusive work culture, helps build team dynamics. The workplace needs to support the overall wellbeing, enthusiasm, and success of employees. Using team-building activities can help.

Pay Attention

You cannot do any of the things mentioned above unless you pay attention to what is going on within the team. If you notice unacceptable behaviour such as bullying or free-riding, take the required steps to correct it immediately. Work on reinforcing positive behaviour such as mutual trust, respect and collaboration. It is the manager's responsibility to take care of the team, and you cannot do this unless you pay attention to them.

Managing Difficult Employees

There will be difficult employees in every organisation. Learning to deal with such employees successfully ensures there is no awkwardness or unnecessary stress. This section looks at helpful tips that managers can use while dealing with such employees or team members.

Criticism Must Be Limited To Behaviour

Whenever dealing with a problematic employee team member,

ensure that the conversation doesn't take on a personal or emotional stance. The idea is not to spark a confrontation, but to resolve the issue at hand. Concentrate only on the employees inappropriate or undesirable behaviour but ensure it is not a personal attack. Critiquing their behaviour is acceptable but don't criticise the person.

Be Open To Feedback

Any conversation you have with the challenging employee needs to be a two-way street. If you want to be heard, you need to reciprocate. If you are unwilling to listen to their comments, the conversation will quickly turn confrontational. Listening to feedback also gives you better insight into the problem and allows you to come to terms with any issues that might contribute to such undesirable behaviour. All you need to do is merely listen, which can improve the situation.

Be Clear

Offering harsh feedback is seldom a pleasant chore for any manager. If an employees behaviour is worrisome or negative, ensure that you provide clear and specific directions on how the set behaviour can be changed. While talking, ensure that your suggestions don't sound defensive or overly critical.

Talk To The HR Department

Schedule a meeting with the Human Resources Department to understand the situation at hand. Talking to others can be helpful if you can't come up with a solution to the problem. If the matter leads to termination, HR can help make sense of the company policies and processes required to terminate such team members employment. If not, they can come up with practical solutions and suggestions to rectify the problem.

Collect Evidence

You need evidence before you can confront the said employee. Without evidence, everything sounds like hearsay. Whenever you notice such performance, make a note of it immediately. Ensure that you maintain a detailed record of the circumstances, and don't forget to add the date. Proper documentation helps recollect specific events and the conversations that took place. These things come in handy, especially if the employee is fired. This reduces the chances for any unpleasant wrongful termination suits.

Work As A Team

Remember, the aim of any conversation you have with a problematic employee is to change their attitude. The solution needs to be mutually agreeable, and you both need to work on improving it. Talk about undesirable behaviours and their adverse effects, and ask them what they think they need to do to improve themselves. Once you both reach a solution, ensure that it is implemented as a team.

Make A Note Of Expectations

Now that you have a solution, make a note of all your expectations from the employee shortly. Also, determine a timeline for such improvement. The plan of action needs to be clear, the timeline specific, and an evaluation framework needs to be created to measure the employees progress. The manager and employee both need to sign this document. Hold on to a copy of this and give another copy to the employee to ensure that the performance can be evaluated later.

Consequences Are Important

The plan of action and the timeline need to work with important consequences. Make it a point that the problem employee or team member is aware of their behaviour's consequences if they don't improve within the agreed-upon time frame. There are severe consequences, from a written warning to withholding bonuses or promotions and even termination in extreme cases. Ensure that you communicate about these consequences to the employee.

Track Progress

The employee will need time to correct their behaviour. During this time, carefully monitor progress and note any improvements or areas where they're still lagging behind. Frequent check-ins and reviews will ensure that you are both on the same page and are working toward rectifying the situation. It also allows you to make changes when required if the employee goes off track. Don't forget to schedule an in-person evaluation to discuss any changes in the situation.

It is important to recognise when the situation is hopeless. Despite your best efforts, if there is no progress or the situation worsens, talk to the HR Department. All that matters is the organisation's wellbeing. If an employees performance hinders this goal, follow the company's termination procedure and immediately cut your losses.

Manage Change And Resistance

Change is the only constant in life. Constant change is the existing dynamic in any organisation. It is important to ensure that there is no resistance while implementing certain changes. Even if the adjustments are desirable, making it is seldom easy. There are different reasons employees resist change. An inherent aspect of change is that it pushes an individual out of their comfort zone. This is challenging, especially when people value stability.

One of the primary reasons there is resistance to change is the fear of losing their job. There is a need to increase efficiency in any organisation, reduce the turnaround time, and ensure the employees are working smartly. All these factors mean the organisation is always on the lookout for downsizing or creating new jobs. This results in fear of job loss.

The lack of proper communication between the management and employees can also result in resistance. Apart from these reasons, the fear of the unknown, the lack of trust in the management, and poor timing are other factors that make employees resist change. As a part of the management team, dealing with resistance and managing change while implementing it is critical.

In this section, let's look at simple tips you can use to implement change effectively while overcoming any form of resistance.

Tackle Opposition

Regardless of your company's policy to deal with or implement any form of change, resistance will always be present. Engaging those who actively oppose the said change is a great strategy. When you do this, it shows those who resist that their concerns are actively heard and understood. It also ensures you can come up with various solutions to resolve the problems in a timely fashion. Allowing employees to offer feedback and share their worries or concerns shows that the management cares for them.

When you are trying to make specific changes, it's important to communicate early. If there is a constant flow of information between the management and other employees, it becomes easier to move forward and ensures that everyone is on the same page. It also shows a free flow of information, honest communication, and clarity.

Another tactic that can be used to deal with resistance is explaining the benefits offered by a proposed change. A simple explanation for "What does this mean for me?" can serve this purpose. By explaining what the employee will gain from the proposed change, it becomes easier to see the bigger picture. Instead of worrying about uncertainties, they can concentrate on the potential gains. Instead of offering a narrow view of what might happen in the future, talking to them about the different ways in which the change is critical will shift their general outlook.

Engage Employees

One of the best ways to overcome any resistance and implement a change is by becoming a good listener. It's not just about giving directives and orders; it is equally important to listen to what the employees have to say. After all, communication is always a two-way street. If all you do is maintain a monologue, it will worsen an existing situation. No organisation can function without its employees. This is why they need to be kept in the loop and on board with any change you desire to make. Seek their feedback while implementing change. If they have any concerns, address them immediately. Unless you effectively read or listen and utilise the feedback you receive, the employees will not feel heard or understood. Try to understand their concerns, address them from their perspective, and engage in active correspondence.

One Step At A Time

Implementing a change is never a one-step process. It practically starts by preparing the employees for change, taking action to enforce the said change, and managing the resultant progress. Apart from this, there is another step involved in this process - to ensure there's plenty of support available for the employees when required.

Effective Communication Is Crucial

A simple yet effective means to overcome any resistance while implementing changes is by effective communication. Explicitly communicate to the employees or team members about what is going on. The combination of formal and informal communication ensures that all the employees receive news about any proposed changes and how they will affect them. Effective communication ensures they understand the organisation's vision, expectations, and goals. It also provides sufficient information to help the employees understand how the change will occur and why it is desirable.

By following the simple tips discussed in this section, you can implement and manage any proposed changes with hardly any resistance. The steps mentioned above will make it easier to ensure that the employees and the management are on the same page about any proposed changes.

How To Manage People With A Short Attention Span

As a manager, you are responsible for dealing with several people employed in an organisation. Since no two individuals are truly alike, you will meet people with various personalities. Ensuring optimal employee productivity is one of the job descriptions associated with a managerial role. While doing this, you realise that there are differences between how people work. Some have an extremely short attention span, while others don't. Learning to deal with employees with a short attention span is crucial to ensure increased productivity, effectiveness, and efficiency. In this section, let's look at some simple tips you can follow to ensure that the workplace is devoid of unnecessary distractions and is conducive to increasing productivity.

According to a study conducted by Philip Lawrence-Spreen et al. (2019), our collective attention span reduces this incredibly connected world. In this study, data were obtained from different sources, ranging from Google books to Google trends, Twitter, and Reddit. It essentially suggests that our collective attention span toward each cultural item is becoming shorter and shorter, with the growing volume of data and information available. The inability to pay attention has a direct effect on the overall productivity and efficiency of an organisation.

Personalise The Information

It is important to personalise the information or data made available to the employees. If they are bombarded with much information, it reduces their attention span. Instead, ensure the knowledge or training you offer applies to them. It needs to be associated with the things they know, how to perform the job, their individual goals, and areas where there is scope for improvement. By measuring their current levels of knowledge and on-the-job behaviour, it becomes easier to offer relevant information. If the information is targeted, the employee will not get overwhelmed by unnecessary data.

Reduce Distractions

The office environment needs to be conducive to focus and growth. If the general atmosphere in the workspace is noisy, it becomes destructive, so try to reduce external distractions as much as possible. It becomes easier to concentrate on the task at hand by eliminating distractions, even for employees with short attention spans.

Simplify The Process

Simplify the process through which employees can get the information they need. Reduce the need for them to hunt for information. When they quickly receive what they need, it becomes easier for them to get on with their work. Quick and personalised material is vital here.

Increase Engagement

We concentrate more on the activities we find enjoyable or the ones that add some meaning to our lives. The simplest way to encourage learning, growth, and development is by ensuring the experience is fun and engaging. An analysis of employees' attitudes and aptitudes helps create personalised programs directed toward increasing their engagement. To do this, you need to step into employees shoes and understand what they seek or desire.

Don't Forget Reinforcement

Since there's plenty of information available, it is imperative to understand that the employees cannot remember everything.

Ensure that critical topics are continuously presented to them. Over a period, it increases their long-term retention.

Seek Feedback

Apart from all the different tips mentioned until now, there is another one you cannot overlook, and it is to get feedback. Since the idea is to increase employees' attention span and retention, it is important to ask them what is and isn't working. Also, seek their feedback about what changes can be made to increase their attention span. It is not just about obtaining feedback. Ensure that you utilise the feedback to bring about desirable changes. This will make the employees feel more understood and heard. All these aspects will improve their overall productivity.

Bridge The Generation Gap

Diversity is a vital aspect of a strong workforce. You will notice several generations with varying attitudes working on a specific task in any organisation. Communication gaps, differences in attitudes, or approaches to different tasks can cause creating a wide generation gap. Bridging this gap ensures that the workforce or employees are all on the same page about the objectives and the methods used to attain them. This is crucial for the overall growth and progress of the organisation and employees.

In this section, let's look at practical tips you can use to bridge the generation gap at work.

Different Channels Of Communication

Using emails has become the unofficial source of primary communication and correspondence in organisations these days. Thanks to ever-growing technology, reaching out to others has become simple. On the downside, it is reducing the scope for personal interactions. Therefore, it is important to ensure the communication channels used don't exclude a particular generation. From face-to-face meetings to phone calls, texts and emails, ensure you include all these communication channels. The older employees might prefer in-person conversations or phone calls more than emails and texts.

The younger ones might favour text, email, or even social media posts. To bridge the generation gap while increasing and strengthening the relationships between different employees, pay attention to the communication channels used. By incorporating other media, you can ensure every generation has space for their preferred form of interaction. It also ensures that all the information is equally distributed and done so in a desirable way.

A Mentorship Program

A simple way to bridge the generation gap is by understanding that each generation offers something unique and valuable. For instance, the older generation of baby boomers has invaluable real-world experience that can provide insights to millennials who are well equipped with the latest technology. By developing a two-way mentorship program, you can create a relationship between different generations where one benefits from others' knowledge and experience. It helps nurture better interpersonal relationships between different employees. This technique is known as reverse mentoring. For instance, the tech-savvy younger employees can teach the older generations about technology, while the older ones can coach the younger peers about face-to-face interactions. Instead of placing a specific generation in the leadership role, it ensures there is a balance and sharing of power.

Never Underestimate The Importance Of Respect

Different factors motivate employees of varying generations. A common factor in all generations is the need for respect. Respect is a two-way street, and by putting respect front and centre, it shows that employees get along well with each other. Everyone feels better when they know they're heard, and their input is appreciated. Employees perform better when they know their knowledge and contributions are appreciated and recognized. Different generations have different reasons why they want to be respected. For instance, Bonnie Monych, a performance specialist, observed that baby boomers want to be respected for their work ethic and maturity while Gen X-ers (1965-80) want this for their self-reliance and millennials (born after 1980) seek recognition for their flexible nature and ability to collaborate and multitask.

Never Assume

Never judge a book by its cover. Remember this idiom when it comes to different employees at work. Let go of any generalisations and stereotypes you might have about different generations. Every individual is different, and by keeping an open mind, you leave room for pleasant surprises. This doesn't mean you shouldn't have an overall understanding of the defining characteristics of each generation. Combine this knowledge making no assumptions about individuals. What works for one person doesn't necessarily work for others. Avoid profiling people based on their age groups and instead, pay attention to their unique personalities and skill sets.

No Age-Segregation

In any group, people gather with others who are similar in age. This is part of human nature. Conversations are easier when the frame of reference is similar. To increase the employees' innovation and productivity in a workspace, different age groups must merge and work as a team. If the generation gap prevents team effort, it will reduce their overall productivity. When the different generations are invested in each other and care for and respect each other, the work environment improves. Concentrate on creating a workspace culture based on recognition. This gives every employee the credit they desire. This increases their internal motivation to work better and together. Also, work on creating opportunities where the employees can appreciate each other. Avoid age segregation and, if you notice it, concentrate on team-building efforts to reduce it. The different tips discussed in the previous section about team-building activities can be used here.

Managing Remote Employees

Situations arise where you need to manage remote employees. Not all employees need to be present at the workplace and in person. When the physical presence is absent, ensuring optimal productivity and efficiency becomes the responsibility of the manager. For instance, the 2020 COVID-19 pandemic resulted in most organisations allowing their employees to work remotely. It is relatively easy to manage individuals at work when they are right in front of you in real-time, but things become a little challenging if that's not the case.

In this section, let's look at some tips you can use to manage remote employees.

Pay Attention To Signs Of Distress

A combination of conversations and indirect observations will help identify any distress the employees might be experiencing. Ensure that you reassure your employees whenever you can to show you understand their challenges and concerns. Show your care and support for them. Encourage regular conversations between employees and management. This ensures their spirit of togetherness and team cohesiveness doesn't fade away.

Provide Resources

Ensure all employees reporting to you are equipped with the required resources to carry on their daily tasks even while working remotely. Whether it is a mobile application or a laptop, ensure they have adequate resources. For instance, how can you expect them to be present for virtual meetings if they don't have the needed technology? Extensive technology or collaborative tools are not required, but don't assume everyone is comfortable working remotely. Virtual communication cannot be perfect, so let go of any notions of perfection. Ensure the communication is professional, respectful, effective, and comfortable. Whenever required, offer them the support and resources to enhance their performance.

Encourage Conversations

Since the employees are working remotely, the need for regular check-ins and conversations increases. Unless there is an efficient and steady flow of information between management and the employees, it will hurt organisational efficiency and performance. As mentioned in the previous chapter, ensuring optimal conversations between management and employees is essential for the successful implementation of changes. By offering them the information they need, it becomes easier to ensure they are in the loop. Also, encourage conversations and communication between employees. When everyone is allowed to express themselves freely, including their fears and concerns, it becomes easier to improve their productivity.

Show Some Trust

The urge to micromanage will increase when you lose the constant visibility of your employees. It can increase your worries or concerns about their performance and even result in frustration. While dealing with remote employees, it is important to keep your emotions in check. You need to act as their support system and provide everything the employees need to do the job well. Instead of giving in to the urge of micromanaging or getting fixated on some assumptions about performance problems you have, it would be better to disengage. By taking a step back and using and establishing a performance management system, you can understand how well the employees are doing and if there is any room for improvement.

Concentrate On Organisational Values

Employees are key stakeholders in any organisation, and this cannot be overlooked. If the employee knows they will be taken care of and supported in the long run, keeping them even while working remotely becomes easier. Ensure that you reinforce and strengthen organisational values and beliefs in your employees. After all, the organisation cannot function without them. Allowing them to understand that the employers and management care for them and are concerned about their wellbeing reduces the chances of employee misconduct while increasing productivity.

Clarity Is Important

Role definition takes a backseat when employees are working remotely. It can make it quite difficult for such employees to concentrate on the activities they need to accomplish or complete. Place more importance on what the employees need to accomplish instead of worrying about the processes. Concentrate on increasing the engagement levels between employers and employees. When the employees know all their effort goes toward attaining the organisational objectives, they feel less anxious about job security. It also makes them feel like an important member of the team.

Output Matters

While your employees are working remotely, their work environment and culture will differ from what they are used to in the office. They might also juggle personal responsibilities while trying to get things done. While working remotely, your primary aim is to ensure that your employees are productive and get things done. Instead of focusing on lengthy processes and time-consuming formalities that merely delay completing tasks, please give them the autonomy to get the desired output. A little flexibility goes a long way while managing remote employees.

More Recognition

Recognition doesn't mean a monetary benefit; even public acknowledgement works. While managing remote employees, ensure that you recognise their effort and accomplishments. Gratitude helps motivate the employees to emulate desirable behaviours again. Unlike the traditional office space, where it is relatively easy to see how well an individual is doing, it takes more attention to understand how the employees perform when the visibility is relatively low. By improving your monitoring techniques and direct relationships with employees, offering recognition becomes easier. This also makes employees feel seen and heard.

Socialising With Your Team

Building, maintaining, and nurturing relationships at work is essential. When you work alongside employees to attain common goals, it gives you a chance to mingle with them on a personal level. Employee relationships commonly develop into friendship and camaraderie as the time they spend together increases. Similar relationships are also fostered between managers and their team members and others they supervise. There is a fine line to tread between leading your employees and being friends with them. The relationship should never lose its professionalism, whether at work or outside. This results in some common concerns managers have about socialising with their teams. Let's look at certain dos and don'ts you need to remember while socialising with your team.

It is important to be friendly with your team members, understand their concerns, and offer support whenever required, but avoid indulging in any form of favouritism. Offering preferential treatment to others can become a severe hurdle, becoming a significant setback for the entire team or department you manage. This can cause distorted perceptions of the manager and create unnecessary trouble. If it makes you seem unjust or unfair to a specific group because you prefer others, it increases frustration and dissatisfaction among other employees. If you don't want to deal with any disgruntled employees in the future, avoid favouritism or any show of preferences.

Boundaries And Work Relationships

If you are quite close with individual employees, chances are you consider them to be your friends. Friends socialise with each other outside work, too. Remember, you cannot forget your managerial position because you have a soft spot for certain people. You are free to maintain friendly relations but avoid socialising outside of work. Even if you are socialising, restrict it to official events. It can raise quite a few eyebrows if you are caught socialising with subordinates at the local watering hole. It shouldn't seem like you are mixing with a particular set of employees because you prefer them over others. In such instances, any accolades the said employee receives will be tainted and viewed as discriminatory treatment. This will land you in hot water with others. If you don't want to get into any trouble with HR later, it is better to maintain your distance.

No Lunch Break With Select Employees

It is a natural human tendency to prefer some over others. After all, birds of the same feather flock together. As a manager, it is crucial to keep this instinct in check. Whether it is a lunch or a coffee break, avoid spending it with only a specific group of employees. If you want to spend time with a particular team member, ensure that you are spending the same time with all your other members, too. If it is good for one employee, it needs to be good enough for others as well. Engage in active conversations and increase their engagement with you. While doing this, don't show any preferential treatment.

No Preferential Treatment

The temptation to give better assignments and projects to someone you have a close bond with is natural. This is what preferential treatment looks like at work. You might want to give someone better assignments or work, which are less taxing because you have positive feelings toward them. When you do this, others will also witness this preferential treatment and resent the directions you give. Whenever you need to assign specific duties responsibilities to individual team members, always based on merit and skills, don't allow your personal feelings to interfere with professional judgments and decisions. The only thing that matters is whether your choices are adding value to your team and the organisation or not.

Never Overlook Poor Conduct

As a manager, you need to ensure that all employees are equal to you. You need to maintain an unbiased outlook toward them. Don't allow a friendly rapport to prevent you from seeing a poor performance or any misconduct. If you turn a blind eye toward these things, everyone at the workplace will expect the same treatment. This will eventually harm the team's performance in the long run. If you notice poor behaviour or performance, address it immediately.

Don't Participate In Office Gossip

The more time you spend with someone, the closer you get. When you become familiar with a person, you get drawn into personal conversations. Avoid doing all this. Do not engage in any form of office gossip. Remember, your job is to regulate all this. If you become a part of the problem, it can become a significant hurdle in your professional life. Avoid indulging in office gossip, internal politics, or peer bashing. Ensure that the office environment is always professional.

Disciplinary Treatment

If disciplinary action needs to be taken against someone in your team, ensure it is done correctly. Don't let your personal preferences bias your judgment. An extreme example of why supervisors should not become involved with any subordinates is that this becomes a hurdle for disciplinary actions. When you consider someone your friend, you end up overlooking their faults. Doing this can harm your team's performance. You will learn more about employee discipline and tips to ensure employee discipline in the later chapters.

Ensure that all your professional decisions are purely based on employee performance, track record, and skills. Regardless of the rapport you share with them, your choices need to be strictly professional. The best way to ensure an impartial and unbiased outlook toward those you supervise is by laying down specific ground rules. Be friendly without becoming a friend. Learn to lead them while listening to their feedback. Avoid socialising with employees outside of work.

Tips For Team Building

Every manager's responsibility is to take care of their team, aid their performance, and attain the team objectives. To do this, it is crucial that the manager and the team are on the same page about what must be done, how, when, and where. The simplest way to get this clarity is by concentrating on team-building activities and exercises. Here are some simple tips you can use to build a successful team.

Understand What A Team Needs

The idea of any manager is to build a fantastic team. You cannot manifest a strong and excellent team out of thin air. It takes a conscious effort of the manager and all the other individuals to make it great. A good team understands its objectives, and the rules of every member are well defined. If there is a hierarchy, all the team members are aware of it, respect it, and are consciously following it. The three other defining traits of a good team are effective communication, unconditional cooperation, and individual development. Whether it is a question, idea, or concern, they are all addressed immediately. Effective communication increases collaboration. When the team functions like a well-oiled machine, achieving team and individual objectives become easier. When the team goals are aligned with the team members' personal goals, achieving them becomes relatively easy.

Leadership Cannot Be Overlooked

Without an effective leader, there's no effective team. The influence exerted by the team leader ensures the team members are performing to the best of their abilities and in the right direction. Being a good leader doesn't mean imposing your authority on others. Instead, it is about fostering a relationship based on mutual respect and honesty. Lead from a place of transparency, so others know what is going on. Even if you aren't with your team at all times, they will approach you if you are open and honest with them.

To become an effective leader, see the bigger picture. Every decision you make needs to be in synchronisation with the broader view and must involve transparency. You need to effectively and efficiently communicate the desired goals with no room for ambiguity. An efficient leader knows how to delegate tasks and responsibilities without giving in to the urge to micromanage. You also need to be friendly and honest without compromising on your authority. This makes you seem more human and allows others to approach you.

Establish A Relationship Between Team Members

A team is only as strong as its members. If your team members don't communicate with one another or cannot get along and work together, it will compromise the team's integrity. It also becomes a significant hindrance while attaining objectives. Your team needs to be self-sufficient. They should be able to get things done, even when you are not around. Your job doesn't end after creating a team and giving instructions. Instead, you need to lead and manage them efficiently, so they achieve the group objectives. The overall productivity increases once they are comfortable with one another.

If they can trust, respect, and confide in each other, they will be more productive.

Therefore, as a manager, it is your responsibility to familiarise the team members with one another. To do this, encourage a couple of teams building exercises to enhance the cooperation between them. Even something as simple as a group lunch or an outing will help the team members interact. By starting conversations about each team member, you're allowing them to understand the other better. If two or more people are working together, conflicts and disagreements are bound to crop up. As a manager, it is your responsibility to avoid such conflicts or resolve them amicably. Be a mediator and help those in conflict reach an agreeable solution.

Get To Know Your Team

Sometimes you need to spend some time and get to know your team at a personal and individual level. Understand the skills, interests, and any weaknesses. Once you understand all this, it becomes easier to designate roles and responsibilities. While doing this, remember that you shouldn't get too chummy with your team members.

Team-Building Activities

Team-building activities offer an excellent platform for the team members to understand and learn about each other. When they work on projects that aren't work-related, they understand each other better as individuals. Some ideas you can use for team building are fundraising projects, outdoor adventures, social events, and indoor activities.

Always Monitor And Review

If you want your team to grow together and become successful, you need to monitor their performance. Unless you do this, you will not know if the team has made any progress or not. Monitoring their performance gives you better insight into their strengths and any areas for improvement. Once you gather this information, the next step is to review it. Scheduling team and personal reviews help ensure the team is moving in the right direction. Make a list of your team's achievements, any changes made, concepts or skills they have gained, areas where they are working well, and the areas where there is scope for improvement. Communicate your feedback to the team. Ask your team for their opinions. This two-way feedback ensures that the team is heading in the right direction.

Managing Different Personalities

No two individuals are alike, and you will come across a variety of personalities at work. A team's success depends on their ability to support each other and work together to accomplish group goals. Apart from ensuring the group attains its objectives, delivers projects on time, and stays focused, a manager has another responsibility. This vital aspect is known as people management. Unless you manage your team members, you cannot ensure they are functioning efficiently or effectively.

As a manager, you need to understand your team. You need to know them in and out. Apart from their strengths and weaknesses, you need to have a good understanding of their basic personalities. If you don't do this, you cannot ensure that you are making the most of their skills. Once you understand your team properly, it becomes easier to put them together and function like a well-oiled machine.

Here are some simple tips you can use to manage various personality types at work.

The first step is to spend a little time understanding what you are getting into. Get acquainted with your team. Most managers forget about this, but it is an essential aspect of your responsibility job description. Try to understand their existing roles, gather information about their previous responsibilities, their aspirations, and get former managers' feedback. The more information you have, the easier it is to understand the rules they are best suited for.

Ensure that you are an excellent role model for your team. Smart work is essential, but so is hard work. There are no shortcuts here. Regardless of your managerial style or the personality types of your employees, hard work is irreplaceable. Stay in touch with your team members, even if they are working remotely. Continually refresh them about the organisational objectives. Help them see the bigger picture. When your team knows their contributions help attain corporate goals, their internal desire and motivation to work better will increase.

Never air your dirty laundry in public. This is one rule no manager must ever forget. If a team member needs to be reprimanded, always criticise in private. Avoid public criticism. Any praise you dole out needs to be in public. By limiting negative feedback to personal interactions, you get a chance to hear the team member out. Apart from this, public criticism has an adverse effect on team morale and can create disgruntled employees in the future. Regardless of the personality type, we all feel good when we are praised and appreciated. If your team does something well, don't forget to complement their efforts. Always concentrate on praising their efforts instead of solely focusing on the outcomes.

Whether it is time to lead or manage your team, some freedom, flexibility, and trust need to be a part of your managerial style. These are the pillars upon which a successful team lies. Regardless of the personality types, everyone enjoys a little freedom and a show of trust. This will make the team players and bring you a step closer to creating a successful team.

Managing Negative Attitudes And Restructuring

The environment at work matters a lot. Positivity is as contagious as negativity. A manager's vital role is to create an effective workplace environment that promotes collaboration and teamwork. A negative attitude can create a significant ripple effect that harms the team's overall productivity and the organisation. Whether it is a toxic or a hostile co-worker or undesirable attitudes, this can significantly influence the collective mindset at work.

In this part, let's look at some simple tips you can use to manage negative attitudes and restructure your team for positivity.

Concentrate On Communication And Collaboration

Effective managers know when to sit down with their employees and talk about their attitude. The only way to build a strong team is through communication and collaboration. Managers not only need to lead, coach, or guide their teams, but should work with their team members. Create a plan of action to improve the overall environment and offer meaningful feedback. Talk to the individual about how their negative attitude or behaviour is harming the team's performance. This might not be a straightforward conversation, but it is vital for your team's health and wellbeing. Talk to the employee about the origin of their negativity and work out together to address it.

Find The Issue

A poor employees attitude might reflect an underlying issue within the organisation. No one ends up with a negative attitude for no reason. There is always a cause, whether or not it is apparent. Negative emotions, inadequate growth, or a toxic work environment can also be a part of a bigger problem. If you notice a hostile atmosphere within your team, talk to them and evaluate their experiences. Ask them for their feedback, have personal one-on-one conversations with them, and identify the issues; unless you recognise the problems, the changes of the negative behaviour or attitude cropping up in the future increase.

Talk About Specific Changes

It can be quite difficult for an employee to change their behaviour unless they know what they need to do and the reasons for the same. Even if your team members know there is scope for improvement but don't know what's to be done or how to go about it, they cannot make any significant or desirable changes. This is where open, honest, and unambiguous communication steps into the picture. Be extremely specific about the changes you want to see if you talk to the employees from that perspective and tell them how to benefit from the said changes; their internal motivation to listen to you increases.

Concentrate On Your Coaching Skills

As a manager, you must keep an open mindset about growth and development. You will need to have a flexible approach while managing your team. After all, a team includes several personality types. If you are equipped with the required skills to have unpleasant or difficult conversations, it becomes easier to rectify the situation. Coaching your employees can help change an undesirable attitude or negative mindsets into positive ones. Similarly, understanding more about different personality types gives you the information required to identify signs of a negative attitude.

Remember, your job as a manager is to ensure that the entire team succeeds, and it is not an individual goal. Whenever you are discussing any workplace issues, avoid pointing fingers. Instead, talk about it from the team's perspective. Always use the word "we" while discussing goals and objectives.

Cultivating A High-Performance Team

The strength and performance of a team depend on the members and their leader or manager. Apart from all the tips discussed in the previous section for team building, here are some additional ones you can use to create a high-performance team.

Mediate Conflicts

Conflicts will crop up, and it is your job to prepare for such situations. Whether it is a difference of opinion or a squabble, nip the conflict in the bud. If you notice something is amiss, solve the problem immediately. Avoid believing that ignorance is bliss. The sooner you tackle it, the easier it is to get the team back on track. If you fail to address a dispute during its initial stages, it can quickly turn into an unproductive team. Creating a positive team environment based on mutual respect and honest communication makes it easier for the team to share their views with no worries. Encourage civil conversations and mediate any discussions about conflicts.

Employee Development Matters

You cannot have a highly efficient and effective team unless the employees focus on their individual growth and development. Personal development is as important as team growth. Avoid micromanaging your team members and equip them with the skills required to resolve problems and grow in the organisation. The more you assist their development, the better the performance your team will yield. When the employees know they're growing, their willingness to contribute to the team increases.

Never Overlook Communication

You cannot accomplish anything in an organisation with no communication. Ensure that employees are kept in the loop about the various changes and developments within the organisation. Alert your team members about any required changes as soon as you get information about it. Your team cannot successfully collaborate and work towards attaining goals if there is no communication.

Set Good Goals

With no goals, it's doubtful that your team will accomplish anything. Regardless of how capable the team members are, they need goals. Plans provide a sense of direction. While setting goals, ensure they are not impossible to attain. A simple acronym you can use to set reasonable goals is SMART. The goals you set should be small, measurable, attainable, relevant, and time bound. For instance, an example of a SMART goal is to "Increase the new consumer rate by XYZ% through boosting sales by XYZ (date)." This goal describes what needs to be done, how to do it, different parameters used to measure progress, and establishing a time limit.

Recognition is a great motivator.

It helps reinforce desirable and positive behaviours. When the employees know their hard work and efforts will be recognised, their desire to perform better increases. Apart from this, ensure that you maintain an optimistic and enthusiastic attitude at work. Your team will follow you, so you need to be an excellent coach, mentor, and leader.

Learning To Lead Vs Manage

All those in a position of authority, whether they are a manager or team leaders, need to switch between managing and leading. These are two qualities that have several advantages but are ideal for varying situations.

In this section, let's understand more about leadership, managing, differences between them, and when to use them.

When you help an individual or a group achieve a predetermined goal, it is known as leadership. The most typical qualities of a leader are the ability to inspire, motivate, and encourage others to pursue a specific goal. The primary focus of leadership is to improve relationships and results by building and maintaining efficient teams that accomplish their goals. On the other hand, management is all about controlling or dealing with individuals and situations. Coordination, organisation, and planning are the three crucial components of management. When you manage a team or a specific situation at work, you are essentially reassessing and tweaking the processes involved to get the desired results.

At work, management and leadership are equally important. These are two different concepts, and understanding each of them ensures you are using them effectively.

Now, let's look at the differences between these two aspects.

Management is often associated with completing a specific task, while leadership is based on a broader vision or mission. When you are managing, you need to effectively follow the rules and ensure the process is going according to a predetermined plan of action. On the other hand, leadership facilitates innovation and creativity. Managers have the primary duty of directing others, while leaders strive to inspire and motivate those who follow them. Management's primary focus is to control situations, people, and the resultant outcomes, while leadership is about inspiring others to think outside the box and get things done. A leader tries to optimise the entire team while a manager focuses on optimising execution of different processes'. Leadership is qualitative, while management is quantitative. The results obtained by the manager are measurable, while that of leadership is intangible.

Now, you might wonder which of these is better. As a manager, you need to shift between leading and managing. There are no hard and fast rules here. So, you need to evaluate the situations independently and decide which style will work. Certain events will call for management, while others need leadership. There will be certain situations where you need to combine both these qualities and work to ensure that the team reaches its goals. Without leadership skills, you cannot inspire or empower your team to attain the goals. Without managerial abilities, you cannot ensure that they are working in the right direction to meet the set goals.

Don't be under the misconception that you need to choose between being a manager or being a leader in all circumstances. Since you are in a position of authority, you get several chances to determine which works better. When you are a good leader, you can effectively influence the behaviour of your team. You have the authority to inspire, lead, and empower them to make the right decisions for attaining a predetermined goal. Managing your team becomes easier if you can lead them effectively and efficiently. If you can influence your team's behaviour through effective leadership and optimising different processes involved in attaining the desired objectives, management becomes more effective. When your team is motivated and engaged, implementing the required policies and enhancing the output's overall quality also becomes easier. It shows that all the employees and team members are focused on specific goals while improving themselves.

This brings us to the next question to determine when you need to lead your team and manage time. By understanding when to use each of these techniques, you can ensure that the team functions as a cohesive unit and powers through any hurdles they face. You can enhance the team's overall performance and output while promoting personal development when you understand when to lead and manage.

When To Lead

While making any changes or introducing an alternative approach, you need to lead your team members. When you know you can trust your team members to complete the task they are given with no micromanaging, leading is a good idea. The same applies during any creative meetings or discussions. When your team members or employees can perform tasks effectively and efficiently and believe in their capabilities, it's time to step into a leadership role.

When To Manage

If there is an emergency at work while training new members, working towards a deadline, and delegating important responsibilities. When the situation requires specific results, it's time to step into a managerial role. When inexperienced team members or new employees need to be taught their responsibilities, you need to be an effective manager. Now is not the time to leave them unsupervised. During these situations, the individuals may require some assistance and supervision, so it is your duty to manage them. When they know what they need to do to complete a task assigned, it becomes easier to achieve the desired objectives. You cannot do this until you are an excellent manager.

You need to lead your team when they are producing excellent results and have superb skills. Step into a leader's role when you believe in their abilities but need to set specific predetermined goals. Once you are aware of your team and are accustomed to their needs, you can approach different situations based on your information. The more time you spend understanding your team, the easier it is to identify and fulfil their needs.

Managing, Participating, And Leading Meetings

Time is an invaluable resource. Sitting through a poorly managed meeting where it feels like nothing significant was accomplished can be frustrating. If you have ever felt like this, there are certain steps you can take to ensure it doesn't happen again. This section looks at some simple tips you can follow to run an effective meeting.

A Meeting Leader

Most of the poorly run meetings are because of the lack of leadership. Before the appointment is scheduled, ensure there is one person who will lead the discussion. Regardless of who the person is, ensure they know what the topic of conversation is. They should be equipped to get the meeting back on track if it goes off track. Leading the forum doesn't mean dominating the conversation. Instead, it merely means setting certain expectations and ensuring the conversation flows in the right direction.

Don't Forget To State The Purpose

Before a meeting is scheduled, ensure there is a specific purpose it needs to serve. Whether it is a regular check-in or a special session, it needs to have a particular purpose or issue to be addressed. Without it, you are merely wasting time, energy, and resources available at your disposal. The purpose of the meeting needs to be stated upfront and communicated to all the potential participants. Without proper communication, it serves no purpose. The most straightforward question you need to answer is why there is a need to schedule a meeting.

Decide On An Agenda

Even a casual meeting needs to have some agenda. The agenda can be informal or pre-established. Make an exact list of different items or topics that need to be discussed and covered. By doing this, you can ensure the meeting is productive. Depending on the formality level or the importance of the discussion and question, consider discussing the agenda beforehand. When you have an exact list of items to be addressed, you can ensure the meeting is productive. This also reduces the chances of forgetting important topics.

Consider The Audience

A meeting isn't effective if it doesn't involve the required attendees. Therefore, it is your responsibility to ensure that all the interested parties are present at the meeting. By knowing your audience or the attendees, you can confirm whether the agenda serves any purpose. If you believe the meeting is essential only for half of your team members, there is no point in having the entire team attend. For instance, if the meeting is about marketing, the research team might not contribute much.

Take Note's

At every meeting, someone needs to make a note of all the discussion points and maintain the minutes of the meeting. This comes in handy in all future meetings associated with a specific topic. You can also use this information if there are any discrepancies in the future. The minutes of the session offer concrete proof about the matters discussed. It also helps ensure that all the points mentioned in the agenda are covered. Once you have delegated this responsibility to a specific individual, others can concentrate on the meeting without worrying about taking notes.

Have A Flexible Schedule

Learn to be a little flexible when it comes to meetings. Apart from weekly check-ins, leave some room for flexibility. If a meeting is important, get on with it immediately. Similarly, if you believe one isn't needed right now, schedule it for later. By changing the schedule, you can prevent the meetings from becoming repetitive or boring. Similarly, while discussing a topic, ensure sufficient time to see things to a logical conclusion. Don't cut brief sessions, especially when the issue at hand is important.

Brainstorming Is Important

If required, set some time aside for brainstorming. A meeting essentially brings people together to discuss ideas. A brainstorming session can help improve the overall productivity and efficiency of the meeting. The best ideas are generated when a group can share their individual opinions.

Time For Discussions

A meeting should not be a monologue. Ensure you are not only an effective speaker, but a listener, too. Allow others to talk and, while they are talking, be a good listener. Usually, leaders and managers forget that others might have feedback and opinions, too. Set some time aside for a group discussion to receive any inputs, ideas, and suggestions.

Pay Attention To How You End The Meeting

At the beginning of the meeting, you need to introduce the agenda. Many people forget it is equally important to concentrate on how the meeting ends. In the end, take a couple of minutes to review all the topics that were discussed quickly. This time can also be used to schedule any follow-ups if required. Summarise the key points of the meeting and discuss the steps of action. If there are individual tasks that need to be completed, don't forget to reiterate.

Get Feedback

Once the meeting ends, don't forget to seek feedback from the attendees. This simple step ensures the meeting is productive. It also allows you to understand where there's room for improvement. If something can be done the next time differently, you now have the feedback to work with.

A little planning and preparation go a long way when making the most of the time and resources available. An unproductive meeting is nothing more than a wastage of an incredibly precious resource, which is time.

Public Speaking

Whether it is a keynote speech or a meeting to pitch a new idea, public speaking is an unsaid part of a leader or a manager's job description. If you cannot effectively and efficiently communicate your ideas, thoughts, and opinions, you cannot get much done.

In this section, let's look at some simple tips and suggestions you can use to improve your public speaking skills.

Understand Your Audience

To improve your public speaking skills, the first thing you need to do is understand your audience. If you don't want to disconnect yourself from the crowd, ensure that what you are sharing is important to them. For instance, if you pitch a new product idea or talk about any changes in the organisational structure, ensure the people you are communicating with are the ones who need to listen to this. Talking about marketing and advertising ideas with the research team probably does not serve any purpose. Therefore, ensure the content you deliver is tailormade for the audience you are interacting with. Place yourself in their shoes and try to think about them. Also, the tone in which you deliver the content needs to appeal to your audience.

Preparation Is Vital

Never underestimate the importance of preparation for a

presentation. Whether it is a keynote address or a presentation, preparation is vital. Rehearse your presentation with multiple groups and ask for their feedback. This is crucial to understand your strengths and potential weaknesses. When you rehearse what you want to say, you can say it more effectively. Practice your speech in front of the mirror. Pay attention to your body language and tone of delivery. This gives you a chance to make the required changes.

Decide What And How To Say It

There always needs to be a central theme to any speech you give. Whether it is a pep talk given to your team members or a new product idea, don't forget to create a central theme or message. Before you make the speech presentation, identify the message, and convey it in ten words or fewer. This ensures your audience is not confused and knows what is in store for them. A general outline of the presentation makes it easier to convey your message effectively and efficiently.

Manage Your Nerves

Public speaking isn't a skill that comes naturally to most, so it is important to manage your nerves. If you seem nervous, anxious, unnerved, or hesitant while speaking, it conveys the wrong message. The simplest way to seem confident is by managing your body language. Avoid slouching, keep your back and shoulders straight, maintain eye contact, and use open body gestures. These simple positions and gestures you make tackle any anxiety or apprehensions you harbour.

How You Speak

Pay attention to how you speak. Regardless of how fantastic your speech is, it will not be effective if you mumble, talk too fast, or aren't clear. After all, what purpose does it serve if your audience cannot understand you? Your voice is the medium you are using to convey the message. An expressive and lively voice helps engage your listeners. When people get nervous, they sputter. Ensure that you speak slowly, pause often to ensure that your audience understands you, and speak clearly. Pay attention to how you enunciate the words and talk. You need to be audible. If you are not loud enough, whatever message you are trying to convey will be lost. To emphasise the message you are conveying, take thoughtful pauses.

Don't Forget About Eye Contact

The importance of maintaining eye contact is an incredibly crucial part of your overall presentation. Whether you are standing on a stage or at the head of the table, ensure that you maintain some eye contact with everyone present in the room. You don't have to fixate your gaze on a specific person or an object. Instead, ensure that you move your eyes and scan the entire crowd. This is a great way to show that you are confident about yourself and your giving speech. When you maintain eye contact, it gives the impression that you are conversing with the audience. It is a crucial part of building and maintaining a rapport. Maintain eye contact with one person for anywhere between 3-5 seconds before moving on to another. If you maintain eye contact for too long or don't maintain it at all, it makes you seem untrustworthy.

Learn From Others

There is a lot you can learn from others. Listen to the speeches given by orators and famous public speakers. Pay attention to the body language, stage presence, and style of delivery. Make a note of all these things and start inculcating or practising them whenever you rehearse a speech. You don't have to copy others, but you can learn a lot from them.

By incorporating these simple tips and suggestions, you can improve your public speaking skills.

Tips For Better Body Language

Communication includes verbal and non-verbal aspects. Apart from the words you say, your body language plays a significant role in overall communication. It is one of the most critical ways in which we communicate with others. Unfortunately, this is one aspect most of us pay little attention to. From your facial expressions to hand gestures and body positioning, there are different aspects of body language. Take a moment and think about it. How would you feel if the person you were talking to slouched, fidgeted constantly, and didn't maintain eye contact? You probably wouldn't feel any confidence emanating from them. Since you are in a managerial role, your body language must communicate your confidence. After all, how can you lead others if you don't feel confident about yourself?

In this section, let's look at some simple tips you can use to improve your body language.

Decide What You Wish To Convey

The way you talk, the gestures you make, your walk, the ability to maintain eye contact, and everything else you communicate about who you are as an individual. First impressions are significant, and they convey more than you can ever imagine. Therefore, the first aspect of improving your body language is understanding what you wish to represent and the distinct qualities you want to convey. Maintaining good eye contact and showing respectful behaviour toward others shows you are reliable and trustworthy. Whether you lean back or forward communicates your interest and involvement in a specific topic. Your physical composure is a representation of your mental state of mind. So, your body language must be in sync with the words you say. For instance, if you pitch a new idea at work, your body language needs to show the confidence you feel. If you cannot maintain eye contact or stare at the wall while talking, it sends a conflicting message.

Open And Closed Body Language

A power pose is the simplest way to show confidence. In certain situations, it can come across as arrogance or defensive behaviour. You need to balance using open-and-closed body language. Ensure that your employees or team members are at ease without giving away too much. While making any major decisions or talking about important decisions, if you keep your head down or don't look at your team, it shows you are doubtful and makes the wrong impression. In such instances, any decision you make will make the team feel anxious and unsure. While talking about ideas, ensure that you keep an open body language. This essentially means you should not fold your arms in front of your body, but keep them by your side in a relaxed and comfortable way. Depending on the circumstances, you need to decide the body language you want to use.

Be Authentic

Nonverbal communication, especially your body language, is based on how you feel about yourself and the audience. There is no one size fits all approach when it comes to nonverbal communication. It is a social experience, and depending on whom you are talking to and what you wish to convey, it will change. For instance, an expansive body language shows authoritative behaviour. When you take up less physical space and display friendly behaviour, it will put others at ease. The nonverbal communication you use needs to feel natural to you. If you are not comfortable with it, it shows. It doesn't mean you cannot work on improving your nonverbal communication skills. From using power poses to matching hand gestures, there are different things you can do. If you are an introvert and try to act like an expressive extrovert, it can come across as fake. Therefore, take stock of your personality and adopt a body language that feels authentic to you.

Build Trust

The simplest way to build trust with others you talk to is by maintaining eye contact. It doesn't mean you have to stare into someone else's eyes constantly. While talking to a specific individual, ensure that you look into their eyes from time to time. It doesn't mean you should stop blinking. Instead, maintain natural eye contact and listen to what they're saying. It helps build trust and shows that you are focused on what they're saying. If you cannot maintain eye contact, it takes away trust and faith in the relationship.

Display Your Listening Skills

When someone is talking to you, ensure that your attention is solely focused on them. Avoid looking at others, distant objects, or staring into space. Avoid crossing your arms or legs while conversing. Be a good listener and pay attention to what they're saying. A simple way to show that you are listening to whatever is being said is by nodding your head from time to time. Even if you don't speak any words, the simple gesture of nodding your head means you are paying attention. While listening to others, sit up straight, don't slouch, maintain eye contact, and use open movements rather than wild gestures with the hands.

Keep Your Hands Open

Whenever you clench your hands or form fists, it increases the tension in your body. This shows that you are on the defensive while talking to others. Even if this is not what you are trying to convey, this is the message that you send across. Avoid doing this. If your body and mind are closed off, you cannot stay open in any conversation. It shows that you are open-minded to all the suggestions, feedback, or ideas that are exchanged. While conversing, keep your hands away from your face. Don't place your hand on your forehead, avoid resting on your hand, and don't cover your face in any way. The safest option is to put your hands in your lap or by your side. Avoid leaning toward too much of the other person. Be mindful of not encroaching into their physical space. This can be constituted as a defensive move and make others uneasy.

Be Mindful Of Your Tone

Another aspect of body language you need to pay attention to is the tone and pitch you use. Your voice conveys a lot. If you are excited about an idea but express this excitement monotonously, it sends a conflicting message. Similarly, if you talk loudly, it can perturb others. Never let your voice betray any anger or unpleasant emotions you might be experiencing. Keep your calm, especially in stressful circumstances. Remember, others are looking up to you for guidance and support. So, you need to maintain your calm.

Common Mistakes To Avoid

Humans are not flawless. Therefore, we are all bound to make mistakes. It might not be an easy thing to accept, but making mistakes is a part of the learning process. After all, even managers are humans and are not infallible. The best way to improve yourself is by learning from your mistakes. That said, there is a lot you can learn from the mistake's others make too.

In this part, let's look at some common mistakes managers make. These are some things that managers aren't taught in business school. By avoiding these mistakes, you increase your overall efficiency as a manager.

Not Understanding The Team

Managers don't exist in a vacuum. Their responsibility is to manage the team they are assigned. Therefore, a manager must manage the team. To do this, you first need to understand your team. If you cannot connect with your team or don't understand them, you cannot do justice to the role you have been given. These days, you can use several forms of communication to stay in touch with your team. From messages to emails and other social media networks, technology is quickly replacing in-person interactions.

Unless you understand your team members on a personal level, you cannot keep them motivated. Understand their ideas, desires, needs, and personal motivations. Talk to them about their interests, struggles, worries, or any challenges. The best way to do this is through one-on-one meetings. By checking in daily with your team members, you can ensure that you are all on the same page about what needs to be done. Spend time and get to know your team.

Maintain A Professional Relationship

In the previous point, it was mentioned that managers need to understand their team on an individual level, but that doesn't mean you get too friendly with them. Don't become too chummy with your team. In the previous section, certain do's and don'ts were discussed about rules a manager must follow while socialising with the team members. Getting to know them doesn't mean you become too involved in their lives. Always maintain a professional relationship. Strike the right balance between friendliness and professionalism. Don't allow others to undermine your authority. Segregate any personal relationships from professional ones.

Not Paying Attention

If you want your team to listen to you, you need to listen to them, too. It is always a two-way street, and you cannot bypass this. This is perhaps one of the most common mistakes that managers make. You are in an authoritative position, but that doesn't mean you shouldn't seek opinions, suggestions, or ideas from your team members. If someone is voicing their thoughts, concerns, or beliefs, ensure that you don't cut them short. By paying attention, you show they are valued and important. Active listening is all it takes to build and maintain a good rapport with your team members.

Don't Micromanage

A good and effective manager knows the importance of not micromanaging the team. Once you have delegated responsibility, don't manage every little detail associated with it. This is a common managerial problem, and many managers are guilty of doing it. This is especially true for new managers who are promoted from a lower rank. It is important to understand that it isn't your job to make life difficult for your team members. Be a mentor and guide your team members to get the desired results. It doesn't mean you should not monitor what they are doing. It merely means giving them the breathing room required to complete the task.

Forgetting To Plan

Not planning properly often results in micromanaging. Don't be a reactive manager. If you try to swoop in and solve any problem or crisis, the team faces without allowing them to solve it themselves, it creates an imbalance in power. The inability to plan appropriately might mean that you end up working longer hours that could have been easily avoided. Instead of being a reactive manager, spend sufficient time and energy creating a proper action plan. If you resolve every crisis the team faces, you prevent them from developing the required skills to solve the problems themselves. Another problem is that you end up burning yourself out by paying extra and personal attention to every little issue that crops up. While creating a plan of action, anticipate any potential hurdles the team might face, resolve them before they can crop up, and help the team members develop problem-solving skills.

Not Setting Properly Defined Roles

You cannot manage your team properly if you haven't given them specific roles and duties. Understand the departmental goals, organisational objectives, and individual goals of your team members. When the employees don't understand what they're doing or the reasons for doing it, and what they stand to gain from all this, it merely increases confusion. If you don't want to create a chaotic team, ensure that you provide them with departmental and personal objectives. Determine the different contributions every member can make toward the set goals while considering their priorities.

Not Showing Humility

Avoid the temptation of going on any unnecessary power trips. Even if you are in an authoritative position, it doesn't mean you need to become power-crazy. Avoid a "My way or highway" approach when it comes to managing your team members. Learn to accept your mistakes, show a little humility, and be an excellent role model for your team. If your managerial style is highly authoritative, it can become ineffective because it takes no account of your worker's thoughts.

Not Standing Up For Your Team

If you want to take credit for all the good your team does, ensure that you will take responsibility when things don't work out too. You need to stand up for your team while interacting with your superiors at work. Don't forget to manage or use your influence while standing up for your team when communicating with others in the managerial chain. You are the mediator between your team members and others in the organisational hierarchy. If you give your team a chance to grow, it will reflect on your managerial abilities.

Not Managing Your Emotions

As the manager, you must manage your emotions properly. Unless you do this, you cannot expect it from your team members. Learn to keep calm even under stressful circumstances. Your team will look up to you for guidance and support. You also need to pay attention to the emotional state of your team members. Developing and showing emotional intelligence ensures everyone stays calm and composed, even in a crisis. If you become unhinged while facing an obstacle, it becomes even more intimidating and worrying for the team. You will learn more about developing emotional intelligence in the subsequent chapters.

Not Providing Feedback

Many managers make a common mistake because they don't offer feedback to their team members or employees. Whenever your team member succeeds, congratulate them and praise them for their success. Similarly, if you notice scope for improvement, offer constructive criticism. Remember, it is important to critique their behaviour and not make any personal digs. Providing feedback is a crucial skill, and it is not just about criticism. If you believe an employee can improve their performance, offer solutions. Ensure the communication between employees and the management is always open and honest. Also, remember that offering feedback is not a one-way street. You also need to listen to any criticism and comments the employees might have to give you.

Don't Assume Money Is The Answer

Avoid assuming that money is the only factor that motivates your employees or team members to work well. Financial reimbursement might be one of the motivating factors, but money is not the answer to all problems. Employees work for recognition, job satisfaction, and a chance to grow and develop within the organisation. If your team members are deprived of all these things, offering monetary benefits doesn't serve any purpose. Also, wrongly believing that financial reward is the only motivational factor in play, you cannot accomplish much as a manager.

It is the responsibility of a manager to ensure that the team reaches its full potential. You are also a part of the team and are not a separate entity. As an important aspect of your job is to ensure that the team succeeds, it is equally important that you grow. Always look for opportunities to grow and become better in the organisation. Learn to set a good example for your team members. If you fail to grow, how can you expect that from others?

Managing Internal Politics

An important yet not so pleasant aspect of a manager's job is to manage organisational politics. Internal politics exist in every company. Organisational or internal politics is the term used to describe any behaviour or activities employees engage in to promote their interests. There is nothing wrong with wanting the best for oneself, but this behaviour becomes problematic when employees advance their interests at the risk of organisational interests. When internal politics are left unchecked, it results in a toxic work environment that slowly but surely erodes employee morale. Friendly competition is healthy and desirable. When left unchecked, competition can become toxic.

In this section, let's look at some simple tips you can use to manage internal politics at work.

Assess The Work Environment

Take some time and assess the work environment. Make a note of employees trying to engage in any form of internal politics to get ahead or not fall behind. Step back and understand the work environment and climate from the employees perspective. Do the hard-working employees get all the praise and perks? Do the self-promoters usually hog the limelight? Before you can address any internal politics, you need to understand what is going on.

Understand The Undercurrents

Forget about the old saying, "Ignorance is bliss," when it comes to internal politics at work. Understand the undercurrents that are constantly flowing. Observe the overall mood of your employees. Become a good listener and encourage them to reach out to you whenever they have any troubles. You need to opt for a proactive approach to tackle and manage internal politics. Whether it is engaging in periodic meetings or informal conversations, stay in touch with your employees. Monitor their overall morale. If you notice any problems, immediately rectify them.

Don't Hesitate To Step In

Disagreements are quite common in the workplace. Regardless of how hard you try, you cannot avoid certain power struggles and petty issues. Managers shouldn't get involved in every battle or squabble. You must not allow these issues to harm your team's overall productivity and prevent them from harming organisational goals. If it feels like you need to intervene, trust your gut and go with it. Schedule a meeting immediately and talk to the parties involved. Play the role of a mediator and help resolve the issue on hand.

If you realise a specific employee is a reason for friction or unnecessary disagreements, talk to that person immediately and fix the issue. Different forms of undesirable behaviours include manipulation, hogging the spotlight, and sabotage that prevents a team from attaining its goals. The sooner you address these problems, the easier it is to fix the situation. As a manager, it is your primary responsibility to ensure that the workplace environment is conducive to productivity and growth.

No Favouritism

Keeping your top performers can help improve your overall productivity, but don't do this at others' expense. Avoid showing any favouritism at work. If there are ground rules established, ensure that they equally apply to all employees and not just some. Perceptions matter a lot in the workplace. If you reprimand employees for their performance, ensure the same rules apply to everyone. You cannot turn a blind eye toward undesirable behaviour displayed by the top performers. If someone's behaviour results in a toxic work environment, avoid showing any preferential treatment and immediately resolve the issue. You need to be fair while enforcing organisational policies. Regardless of the person, you are dealing with, it is always better to stick with the policies, procedures, protocols laid down in the organisation.

As a manager, you are in a position of power and authority. With power comes responsibility. You are responsible for making good choices, staying calm in unfavourable circumstances, and staying positive. Your team learns their attitude cues from you. Therefore, ensure that you are practising all that you preach. Maintain a positive attitude, avoid indulging in unnecessary gossip, and never criticise others openly. By following these simple protocols, you are teaching your team members excellent and desirable behaviour. Be an exemplary role model, and the chances of others following you will increase.

CHAPTER 6: WE SHOULD TALK ABOUT HUMAN RESOURCES

Human resources is a term used to describe any individual working within an organisation by trading their knowledge, skills, or other capabilities in exchange for compensation regardless of whether they are part-time or full-time employees. Most common functions of human resources management include hiring, interviewing, and training employees, disciplining and firing them, onboarding, performance management, and organising and developing a work culture.

In this section, let's explore more about the role a manager plays in HR.

Hiring And Interviewing

An important job played by a manager is hiring and interviewing potential employees. This leads to the question: how do you know who the perfect candidate for the job is? There are several strategies and tips you can use while hiring and interviewing potential employees.

Switch Things Up

Instead of a typical interview with its predictable choreography, change things up a little. Apart from asking questions which are obviously expected, such as "What are your strengths?", "Where do you see yourself in five years?", "What is your biggest failure, and what are your weaknesses?" These are some questions that are almost always asked in regular job interviews. Apart from this, you can also expect some small talk about common interests or a shared past, if any. None of these topics gives much of an insight into the employee you are hiring. Even if their references check out, they might not live up to the workplace's required standard once on the payroll. This happens more frequently than anyone would care to admit.

An important aspect of human resource management within an organisation is to hire the right people for the right job. If an individual's skills are not in sync with the job requirements, it will harm the overall productivity, quality of work, and efficiency of the organisation.

Remember, it's not just the managers who know the format of a standard interview. Even the candidates prepare themselves for these basic questions. Therefore, it's time to get a little creative and look for innovative ways to pose questions that will help get a better understanding of the person you are interviewing. Instead of asking them about their weaknesses, place them in a challenging situation that reveals their traits. Why don't you get your other employees or team members to help you here? If you are hiring a specific team member, ask the existing members what they think of the potential candidate.

Step Away From The Desk

You will better understand the candidate if you don't restrict yourself to a regular desk and chair interview. Get away from the desk and watch how the candidate behaves. Two important qualities you need to look for while sizing up potential job candidates are their interest in the work carried on by the organisation and how they treat others. You get a better sense of their personality by taking them away from the office or the conference room and can see how they interact and behave in the real world. You can also give them a tour of the workplace and show them around.

Pay attention to how they interact with others, body language, and the questions they ask. Another idea you can use is to take your candidate out for a meal or coffee. Pay attention to whether the potential job candidate is polite to the servers, maintain eye contact, the ease with which they hold a conversation, and so on. These are some simple gestures and behaviours that give you an in-depth understanding of who a person truly is.

Unusual Questions

If you want the candidates to open up or understand things that make them tick, asking unusual questions helps. Chances are, you will run into candidates who are smart and are aware of different techniques they can use to turn any negative points conveniently into positive traits. They also find it extremely difficult to admit their weaknesses, and they may believe vulnerability reduces their desirability for an organisation. Instead of common questions, if you want to know and get a better sense of the candidate you are interviewing, ask some unusual ones. That doesn't mean you should ask them brainteasers. Instead, you need to get creative about the questions you ask. You can ask the candidate about their natural strengths. Ask them what animal they would choose to be and their reasons for that choice. Apart from this, you can ask them about the most common misperception others have about them. You can ask several things to truly understand where the candidate comes from and assess their thinking process. For instance, by asking them about the distinct qualities or traits they admire in their parents, you get a sense of their family. Become a smart interviewer and ask unusual questions.

Most of these questions cannot be answered if the candidate is not self-aware. Employees who lack self-awareness cannot be valuable assets in an organisation. Self-awareness is crucial because it teaches you about your strengths, weaknesses, and vulnerabilities. Unless you acknowledge all these things, the chances of growing in life are relatively small. Self-awareness also teaches you about the mind required to navigate tricky situations and skills all employers look for in potential employees.

Writing Job Descriptions

One of the most critical roles of an HR Manager is to write compelling job descriptions. A job description helps identify unique abilities or skills required for a specific position within an organisation. It efficiently conveys the message about other things that are involved or required for a particular job. It allows you to describe the minimum qualifications for a specific position. Even if it does not seem like much, writing an adequate job description helps find the right person for the right job.

In the next part, let's look at some simple tips you can use to write compelling job descriptions.

Writing Job Details

A common mistake many people make is that they believe job postings and job descriptions are the same. A job posting is usually an external-facing document that serves as an advertisement for an organisation's available position. On the other hand, a job description involves a detailed record of required skills, responsibilities, knowledge, behaviour, education, and other areas necessary to carry out a specific job efficiently. Therefore, don't make the mistake of using these terms interchangeably.

While writing a job posting, you are free to include information about the organisational culture, perks it offers, and all the benefits of a specific role. It essentially comprises the bare minimum facts describing the job and is a recruitment tool. A job description serves a dual purpose. It is used as a tool for talent management and serves as an official record of a specific job's requirements. The more details included in the job description, the more it serves as a record of information useful for management and employees.

Pay Attention To The Content

This includes writing style, and the content makes all the difference between a good and a great job description. Adding competencies required for a specific job in clear and measurable terms lays down a solid foundation for good job descriptions. Competencies refer to the required and desired skills and behaviours for successfully performing the job. Adding competencies to a job description can be used as a tool for talent management, and its application goes beyond the hiring process. The three types of competencies included in a job description are knowledge, skills, and behaviour. All these three categories include general or organisational requirements and specific requirements.

Standardised Descriptions

By establishing starting standards, you can ensure consistency in all the job descriptions written for an organisation. For instance, some managers might prefer listing out the basic facts of a job, while others include vague information and language. If there is no consistency, the quality of the job description suffers. It also reduces the ability of an employee to transfer the competencies from one team to another seamlessly. By establishing a uniform job description format and standardised descriptions for positions, the hiring process improves. You can also increase the quality of the hires while making the entire process fair and transparent. Writing an adequate job description and creating a standardised definition for positions are crucial steps that cannot be overlooked.

Compliance Requirements

When a job description is written correctly, it serves as a record of all the job's different responsibilities and duties. These apply to the employee and the employer. By getting an employee to sign off on the job description, you can use it as a part of the organisation's compliance management strategy. If there are any disagreements about their responsibilities, performance, or even accountability of a specific role within the organisation, the job description can be used as a compliance tool. When in doubt, you can refer to the job description to understand what is and is not included within a role's requirements.

Discipline The Employee

One of the most common aspects of human resources everyone is aware of includes disciplining employees. Workplace discipline is paramount to overall productivity and professionalism maintained within an organisation. This is also a vital factor that influences the workplace or organisational culture. When employees are disciplined, their ability to stay focused on the goals or tasks allocated to them while making the most of the resources available increases. Discipline helps increase productivity. Employees might engage in undesirable behaviour or display some negative attitude. In such instances, it is the responsibility of the manager to step in and discipline employees. This section lets you look at some simple and valuable tips managers can use while disciplining their employees or team members.

Always Start With Training

The simplest way to ensure that all the employees in an organisation are well disciplined and do not cross any lines or violate organisational rules or policies is training. Training can be offered during the induction process or after they've gone off track. If you want to rectify an employees behaviour, reassign them to different tasks, and implement a specific training program. Afterwards, evaluate any of the problem points. Reassigning your employees with the desired training serves as a reminder of the activities that got them off track and the ones that helped them get back on it. Training is a preventive and curative measure. Ideally, it is better used as a preventative measure.

Policies And Consistency

If there are any expectations, ensure that they are given to the employees in writing. Apart from this, there need to be obvious consequences if the said expectations are not met. If you handle employee discipline by establishing robust policies, it becomes easier. By doing this, it seems as if a penalty is a natural consequence of the behaviour. Once you have these policies in place, you need to maintain consistency. As a manager, ensure that you do nothing that undermines your credibility. While dealing with employee discipline, ensure that you treat all employees equally and do not show any favouritism. Consistency in implementing robust discipline policies helps improve employee discipline.

Always Have Documentation

While handling employee discipline, you must note everything you have coached the employee about before the discipline process starts. Document everything you wish to discipline the particular employee about, so there is an exact reason there is a need for discipline. Documentary evidence also creates proof that the said employee violated one of the organisational policies. This comes in handy in the later stages, especially if it results in suspension or employment termination.

Improvement Is Important

With employee discipline, it's always better to use a corrective approach. Punishment might not always work, and it is better to have a detailed plan of action that can correct the employee's behaviour. From performance-related one-on-one conversations with the employee to suggest some changes in the employees' attitude and behaviour, different things can be done. Punishment does not serve any purpose. For instance, punishment shows what is not desirable, but it doesn't show what should be done or is appropriate. Instead of punishing the employees when they do something that you don't want them to do, it is better to show them what they should do.

Individual Perspective

Employee discipline needs to be individualised. What might work for one doesn't work for another employee. Unless the discipline policies cater to each employee at a personal level, it might not be sufficient. Employees might respond to pep talks, while others need a firmer approach. To ensure that employee discipline is optimised, get to know the employees you are supervising.

Apart from personalising the disciplinary tactics, it is crucial to treat all your employees as adults. It essentially means the focus of discipline needs to be on informative conversations instead of punitive approaches. By using phrases such as "This can cause disciplinary action," the conversation sounds threatening. Instead of threatening, scaring, or condescending, it is better to have a mature and honest discussion with the concerned employee. You can take this a step further and ask the employee how they think they can improve themselves. By considering their feedback and suggestions, you can create a better plan of action to rectify the situation.

The Rule About Bad Behaviour

As a manager, it is your responsibility to monitor your team's behaviour and productivity constantly. If you notice any undesirable or bad behaviour, try to rectify it immediately. Do not let this problem grow and become unmanageable. While you do this, you need to be consistent about implementing disciplinary policies and always treat your employees equally. Do not be biased towards one and let them get away without accepting responsibility for their actions or behaviour. Remember, the entire team is watching how you deal with different employees.

While implementing the different tips and suggestions discussed in the section, understand that discipline always comes from within. Regardless of all that you do, it will not be effective unless the employees are willing to correct their behaviour.

Firing People

There are several unpleasant conversations and confrontations you need to undertake as a manager. One of the most dreaded conversations is when you need to let an employee go. In the previous section, you were introduced to several disciplining techniques that can ensure employee discipline within an organisation. At times, despite all of this, the best thing you can do, keeping the organisational goals and values in mind, is to let an employee go. If you ever have to deal with such a situation, here are some tips that will help make this conversation go as smoothly as possible.

Time To Change

If you have any complaints about the employee's performance, behaviour, or general attitude, the first step is not to fire them. Unless there are specific serious changes or restructuring of the company, you should never start a conversation about employment termination. If their performance is lacking, you need to give them a chance to rectify it first. To get started, discuss with the employee and point out the behaviours that need to change. After the behaviour and the reason have been identified, create a plan of action to rectify the situation. After this, give the employee 30 days to change, and if you don't see any changes after the grace period, you can end their employment.

The Place And Time

If you are firing an employee, never do it publicly. This can be demoralising, demotivating, humiliating, belittle, and highly unprofessional. Find a quiet and private space where you can have this difficult conversation with the employee. While talking about an employees termination of employment, ensure that you are 100% engaged in the conversation. There is no specific time or date that is ideal for firing an employee. It is a personal preference and choice. Depending on the circumstances in the organisation, get on with it whenever you want to. If you are unsure of what needs to be done or how to go about it, consult the HR Department. You can also seek feedback from your team about this action.

Be Abundantly Clear

This conversation will not be pleasant, it will be awkward, and you might be in a rush to get it over with. But you need to ensure there is no ambiguity or scope for hope left after this. You are firing the employee, so now is not the time to cushion the blow with a few compliments. You can be polite without creating ambiguity. If you tell the employees, they have been doing a good job, offer a compliment about the work, and then tell them they are fired, it sends a conflicting message. Even though it is an awkward conversation, ensure that you clearly and unambiguously convey the point that their employment is ending. There is no room for them in the organisation.

It might sound brutal, but with no clarity here, it results in more confusion and chaos.

No Pet Peeve Phrases

While firing an employee, don't worry about sugar-coating what you are saying. It can be tempting to do this, but restrain yourself from doing this. Common phrases that can typically arch the employee include, "I know how you are feeling," "You should have known this," or "Even if it hurts right now, I know you will soon realise this is the best thing to have happened to you."

None of these phrases are helpful. They offer little or no comfort to the employee and are often seen as condescending. If someone is processing important news such as losing employment, their emotional state is fragile. In such instances, these phrases merely increase the frustration and further the hurt they feel. If you are uncertain of what to say, the best thing you can do is not say anything.

Don't Argue

The chances of an employee becoming defensive or angry are relatively high in such instances. Don't become hostile when the employee becomes hostile. If the employee is defensive, there's nothing to gain by pointing out the different times they did not meet the expectations. Doing this will merely escalate the situation. Regardless of all that the employees have said, stand your ground, especially if your decision is right for your team and the organisation. Stand for many choices, even when the employee thinks they can make things right. Remember, you have already allowed them to do this. It was their failure to do this, which has landed them here today. Regardless of any pleading to reconsider the original decision, it is vital that you do not go back on that decision. If you go back on this decision, it will make you seem weak and result in a toxic relationship between you and other staff members.

Suggestions For Appraisals

A simple and effective way to measure employees' productivity and impact is through regular performance reviews or appraisals. That also forms the basis for any disciplinary proceedings or terminations against an employee. Even though this might not be something you are interested in, it is crucial. Properly conducted appraisals help identify the areas where there is a need for improvement while offering employees the recognition they desire and deserve.

In this section, let's look at some simple tips you can use to get through the appraisal process.

The first step is to establish and track measurable goals.

If you want to review an employees performance, you need to

develop a foundation for that. It essentially means the organisation's objectives and individual employees' goals need to be realistic, measurable, and time-bound. This is where setting SMART goals steps into the picture. This acronym stands for specific, measurable, achievable, relevant, and time-bound goals. While drafting the plans for employee appraisal, use the SMART technique. For instance, it helps you identify the specific task that needs to be completed or the actions required to be taken to achieve a particular goal. Make a note of the type of information that will be used to track employee progress. Apart from this, there also needs to be a standardised process for recording and collecting data. You need to ensure the company's and individual's goals are achievable. Therefore, see whether the employees have the required skills and resources to achieve their set goals. Apart from that, the goals need to be time bound and relevant. If the plan is not aligned with the organisation's broader objectives or there are no deadlines within which they need to be achieved, it's of no purpose. While laying the foundation for an employee appraisal, don't forget to follow this step.

Important Feedback.

If there is important feedback or suggestions to your team and employees, do so immediately. Do not wait until the scheduled performance appraisal. When they know what is expected of them, it becomes easier for them to monitor performance. By giving them opportunities to rectify that performance before the appraisal, productivity can increase. It also creates a positive work culture. If anything noteworthy happens, record it. Whether it is good or bad, this documentation helps with performance appraisal later. As a manager, you need to continuously provide feedback and suggestions to ensure your employees' optimum productivity.

Different values that play a crucial role during performance appraisal include honesty and transparency. Offer helpful feedback and suggestions that can be easily incorporated into your employees daily routine to optimise their productivity. Ensure that you keep an open mind during the review. Regardless of how much you favour an employee, do not make things personal. Be direct, kind, and firm.

Since organisations are continually changing, the goals established for employees will also change. If this happens before the review period, take into consideration the changes and employee performance. Avoid a fixed approach when it comes to employee appraisals.

Effectively Manage Conflicts

As a manager, dealing with conflicts and the workplace is an unavoidable part of your responsibilities. The inability to cope with conflict creates a hostile or even toxic workplace. It also reduces employee and team productivity. Conflict resolution is a crucial skill for all managers and leaders alike. Let us look at some practical and straightforward steps you can use for conflict resolution.

With conflict resolution, it is critical to remember that the primary aim is to maintain positive working relationships. In the end, it is about improving and maintaining the high-quality performance of all your team members. Learn to resolve the conflict without allowing it to hinder your team's quality of output.

At times, it can be challenging to reach a mutually agreeable solution. In such instances, it is better to agree to disagree. Disagreements are bound to crop up. By encouraging your team to expect them, it will not catch them off guard.

It is not always necessary that all the disagreements are discussed. There will be some instances where issues are not discussed. As a manager, you need to build trust and earn the confidence of all your team members. By maintaining open and honest communication policies, you can encourage your employees to confide in you. Learn to become an active member of the team. Apart from this, become adept at reading nonverbal cues about any growing disagreements within the team. Whether it is a quick flash of anger or the constant rolling of eyes, paying attention to these cues will rectify the problem during the initial stages.

As a manager, you need to maintain a neutral perspective in times of conflict. Do not favour any one employee. Instead, view it from the perspective of all the parties involved. By doing this, you get a better sense of what is happening, its reasons, and the most effective means to deal with it.

While resolving a conflict, do not speak for others. Do not assume what others might feel or think. Instead, merely state your views and opinions. You need to act as a mediator and facilitator to ensure all conversations about conflict resolution go in the right direction.

It is crucial to pay attention to what you say, how you say it, and any underlying meaning. A simple disagreement can quickly escalate into a nasty argument when emotions get the better of you. Learn to keep things professional and always use a calm voice. Don't encourage any of the employees to put others down or tell tales. The conversation about the conflict needs to be associated with the issue at hand. You need to stay on point and don't allow employees to bring other arguments into the arena.

Avoid using any form of print media while handling a conflict. It might sound like a simple solution. After all, it hardly takes a couple of minutes to draft an email about a specific conflict. Unfortunately, this method of conflict resolution increases the risk of misunderstandings and ambiguity. It is always better to have personal meetings to resolve disputes and disagreements.

Whenever you are resolving conflict, ensure that you always listen before speaking. Do not listen to point out flaws in someone else's ideas, thoughts, or opinions. Learn to be calm, become a good listener, and respond empathetically.

CHAPTER 7: WHEN IT'S NOT ABOUT TEAM AND BUSINESS. IT'S ABOUT YOU!

It can be overwhelming to transition to a new role as a manager. It is a significant achievement in your professional life. That said, balancing professional and personal life is vital. When you are not concentrating on your team or worrying about organisational success, spend time improving yourself. After all, you cannot help others if you don't focus on self-development and growth. You need to set a good example for your team and others you supervise. Make sure that you follow all the advice and suggestions you offer your employees.

Self-Development

You are responsible for your team development and growth, but concentrating on self-development is important. Remember, your development is wholly and solely your responsibility. Unfortunately, even though most managers know this, they fail to do anything about it. It can be relatively easy to put self-development on the back burner when there's a lot on your plate. Therefore, it is crucial that you prioritise self-development instead of leaving it to luck.

Let's look at some tips you can use to develop yourself. Never limit your thoughts to your current work and always dream bigger.

Don't get too absorbed in the managerial role that you forget about developing yourself as an individual. If an employee came to you seeking advice for self-development, what would you suggest? Now, try following the same advice. Ask yourself what it will take to fully invest your potential and work on actively developing your life. The first step you can take toward training the subjective is by engaging in a self-appraisal. Make a note of your strengths, weaknesses, the different opportunities available, and any hurdles you might face, preventing you from making the most of those opportunities. Take into consideration your regular work and look for areas where there is scope for development. Make a list of all the different professional skills and qualifications you can gain to work your way up the managerial chain.

Instead of blindly conforming to whatever skills or qualifications the organisation might tell you, select an area you wish to develop. Both these things might be the same. If they are not, take some time and choose to do it. If you believe learning a new skill or improving your existing capabilities will help you move up the corporate ladder, go for it. Now that you have identified your weaknesses, it can be tempting to concentrate all your time and energy on overcoming them. Don't get so caught up in this process that you don't work on harnessing your strengths. If you're good at something, make yourself better while simultaneously working on your weaknesses.

Take some time and think about your dreams and aspirations in life. Visualise the life you want to live five years down the line. Make this virtualisation as straightforward as you can. Make a note of all the different things you wish to accomplish during this lifetime. Start prioritising them in order of importance. Once you are aware of all this, it's time to take action and focus your energy and resources in the right direction. Accomplishing the significant goals in life is not a sprint. Instead, it is a marathon. You need to work toward learning daily. Therefore, make a note of all the different activities and tasks you can perform daily to aid your development.

Learn to celebrate your victories. Even if they are small, they are yours, and they need to be celebrated. If you don't take pride in your account placements, you set a poor role model for your team. Taking pride in your accomplishments and achievements is a sign of self-confidence and strength. It doesn't mean you need to boast about your achievements to anyone who is listening. Instead, it means you appreciate all that you've accomplished.

Do not become too complacent and content with the way things are right now. If you become incredibly comfortable in the present, the chances of growing in life reduce. After all, growth doesn't take place within the comfort zone. Therefore, create an attitude of healthy dissatisfaction. This ensures that you are always motivated to improve yourself and do better. It doesn't mean you need to be extraordinarily critical or harsh of yourself. It merely means you don't stop learning and growing.

Coping With Stress

Stress has become a constant companion in the fast-paced and hectic world we live in. Managers have several responsibilities, rules, and duties they need to discharge. All of this can become quite stressful. If you cannot manage your stress, you will eventually burn out. It can also result in disengagement and reduction of productivity. When you are stressed, your ability to think and make the right decisions reduces drastically. This will reduce your productivity and quality of work. There will be several stressful circumstances you will face. In such instances, if you let stress get the better of you, it will make the situation worse. By using these simple strategies, you can effectively reduce any stress you experience at work.

Define Your Expectations

In the previous chapter, you were introduced to several practical and helpful suggestions and tips to become an effective communicator. A simple way to reduce any stress you experience is by effectively communicating about your team members and employees' responsibilities. Don't forget to communicate about their performance expectations. While doing all this, remember, there is no room for ambiguity. When the employees and the members are aware of all that they need to do to satisfy the requirements associated with their job, the chances of complacency are reduced.

Delegate Responsibilities

If you want to be an efficient manager, you need to delegate all your responsibilities and prioritise tasks to concentrate on. After all, you only have limited time and resources to dedicate to various tasks and activities. Don't micromanage your team and instead trust their abilities to get things done. This helps improve the team's productivity, confidence, and skills.

Time Management

Believe in your employees and have faith in their abilities to complete tasks effectively and efficiently. Time management is a crucial skill in all aspects of your life. Prioritise the tasks and order of their importance, establish timelines to accomplish them, leave room for unexpected changes, and delegate responsibilities. When you know your team or employees will get things done, it will reduce any stress you experience.

Plan Daily

If you want to get a head start, outline your priorities daily. Communicate these priorities to your team. If they know what's to be done, they will get it done. By visualising the daily objectives your team needs to accomplish, creating a plan of action to achieve them becomes easier. When they are aware of their individual goals, the chances of success increase, and it also improves the team's overall efficiency.

Regular Breaks Are Important

The human body and mind are not infallible machines. If you want to perform effectively and efficiently, you need to take breaks. If you don't take any breaks and continually work, you will burn yourself out. Apart from this, it will reduce your productivity. If you don't want to get overwhelmed by all the work, you need to plan your day so that you have time to take breaks regularly.

Work-Life Balance

Striking the right balance between professional and personal life is crucial for your overall wellbeing. It's not just your productivity that's affected when you don't have this balance; it increases stress, frustration, and feelings of disappointment. If all your time in energy goes toward managing your official responsibilities, you'll be left with little or nothing in your personal life. Remember, in the previous chapter, finding the right balance is vital to prevent burnout and engage mental awareness? This applies to managers too. Here are some simple tips you can use to strike the right balance between work and life.

Plan To Recharge

As a manager, you need to juggle multiple responsibilities and play different roles depending on circumstances. To do all this efficiently and effectively, you need plenty of energy. It's not just physical energy. You need to be emotionally and mentally healthy. Therefore, taking some time to recharge your batteries is essential for all managers. When things start to get too hectic, do not forget to take a step back and recover. Schedule at least two 15-minute breaks daily. Take a 15-minute break during the morning and in the afternoon. These breaks should be taken in addition to all your lunch, washroom, and coffee breaks.

Start Of The Day Process

As soon as the day begins, take some time to create a checklist of all the different things you need to do before getting on with your daily responsibilities. By doing this, you can ensure that you accomplish everything that you are supposed to do. Chances are you forget things to do something else because you were overwhelmed by the tasks. By creating a start of the day process, you reduce the risk of forgetting important tasks. It is essentially your start of the day checklist.

Here are some jobs you can include in this process. Review your weekly calendar goals, check your inbox, reorganise your workspace, keep things tidy and organised, scheduled breaks, and make a list of tasks you want to accomplish on the given day. By reviewing the simple last, you can get started with your day on the right footing. It also helps you seamlessly move from one task to another without wasting time thinking about the tasks that need to be completed.

End Of The Day Process

Before you go home or stop working for the day, take some time, and review your start of the day process list. Check everything that you have completed off the list. Reviewing this list helps you wind down and prepare for the following day. When you know all the different things you have and have not completed, you get a better sense of managing your time and resources. Chances are, it might help create an official plan of action to accomplish more on the following day.

Organise Your Workspace

A cluttered workspace can reduce your productivity and increase distraction. If you want to concentrate effectively and efficiently on the task at hand to improve your work and product quality, keep your workspace tidy and organised. Yes, it is time to go to Mary Kondo in your workspace and follow minimalism principles. Minimalism is a simple concept that suggests that anything that does not add any meaning or value to your life needs to be discarded. By following this rule at the office, you can create a well-organised workspace free of clutter and junk. It helps concentrate only on the tasks that require your attention without getting distracted by everything else. This is a great way to reduce any stress you experience.

Plan For Holidays

Every day, you need to take a couple of breaks to recharge your body and mind to work better. These breaks help improve your concentration motivation and enable you to stay focused on a given task. Similarly, you need to plan for vacations too. Regardless of how overwhelming or hectic work seems to get, you need a break.

Without breaks, you cannot improve your overall productivity or efficiency. By planning for a holiday, you are effectively giving yourself a goal to look forward to. When you know all the hard work you are putting and will pay off later, your motivation to do better will increase. It also ensures you are striking the right balance between your work and personal life.

Personal Discipline

Self-discipline is a valuable trait in all aspects of your life. It helps you accomplish things and work toward your goals, even when you don't want to. It becomes easier to stay on the right track and avoid any distractions when you have clear goals. This is by self-discipline steps into the picture. It promotes you to take positive action daily, which brings you a step closer to your objectives and goals. As a manager, you must model good behaviour. If you want your employees to be disciplined, the Buck starts with you.

Here are few suggestions you can use to increase your self-discipline.

Areas For Improvement

If you are honest and take some time for self-introspection, you will realise your strengths and weaknesses. It helps you identify the areas of your life where you are doing well and where there is scope for improvement. If you have a growth mindset, you realise it is always a scope for improvement. Think about different habits or qualities you want to improve, such as reducing distractions at the workplace, overcoming procrastination, or improving your time management skills. Once you know the areas where there is scope for improvement, taking corrective action and implementing changes becomes more effortless. If you are struggling to identify any improvement areas, you can talk to your peers at work, friends, and even family members.

Defining Your Expectations

Based on the areas of improvement you've identified, you need to establish specific goals and expectations. Create a plan of action to improve your work performance and all the other desirable qualities. While working on improving yourself, don't forget to establish realistic goals. For instance, if you have realised that your prioritisation skills are not good, it is time to improve. Starting immediately, make a list of different tasks and their deadlines. Estimate the time taken for each of these tasks and create a schedule for every workday. By defining your expectations, it becomes easier to establish realistic and achievable goals for yourself.

Achieve Your Goals

Your job doesn't end after establishing your goals. These goals will amount to nothing if you don't push yourself to achieve them. There will be days when you don't feel motivated to accomplish the tasks you set out to do. In such instances, remind yourself of all the different benefits you stand to gain by completing the task. During the initial stage, this might not be a straightforward thing to do. With practice, you will get better at motivating yourself to achieve your goals. Whenever you accomplish a goal, it increases your confidence and motivation to do better.

Measure Your Progress

Now that you are making a conscious effort to achieve your goals, it is important to track your progress. Therefore it is crucial to set real and achievable goals. By establishing specific parameters that help measure your progress, you can identify areas for improvement while working on your strength. When you can see the distance you have covered, your self-discipline to keep going increases. It also ensures you are on the right track and are not getting distracted.

Don't Forget To Reward Yourself

Whenever you achieve a goal, don't forget to reward yourself. This reward doesn't have to be anything significant. Even if your achievement is small, it is worth celebrating. Learn to take pride in your achievements and accomplishments. Whenever you celebrate your achievements, it fuels your motivation to do better. It is also a sign of self-respect and love. Regardless of the goal you have accomplished, congratulate yourself.

Keep Learning

There will be days when it feels like everything works favourably, and you are on the right track. Similarly, they will be days when it seems like nothing is going as planned. In such instances, accept your obstacles and learn from them. Every setback is a learning experience. Make a note of your mistakes and the different steps you can take to prevent them in the future. Learn from your past challenges and stay on the right track. You also need to keep up with changes within the industry. This is one reason constant learning is an unspoken part of every manager's job description.

To improve your self-discipline, get a head start on your day by accomplishing minor tasks. Do not ignore self-care and pay attention to your mental, emotional, and physical health. Avoid getting distracted and stop multitasking. Learn to manage your stress by following the different types discussed in the previous sections. Similarly, ensure that you give yourself sufficient breaks to improve your productivity.

Upgrade Your Emotional Intelligence

Emotional intelligence or emotional quotient is the ability to manage, understand, and utilise your emotions positively to reduce stress, communicate effectively, diffuse conflicts, and empathise with others. Your emotions and feelings play a vital role in your thought processes. What you felt and what you experienced regulates your thoughts. Since your thoughts regulate your actions and behaviours, they directly affect the quality of life you live. A common mistake many people make as they prioritise analytical intelligence over emotional intelligence. Upgrading your emotional intelligence improves your people skills and ensures that you have complete control over your emotions. If you allow your feelings to regulate your life, you will quickly be overwhelmed, and the chances of making sound decisions will reduce.

Next, let's look at some ideas you can use to increase your emotional intelligence.

Pay Attention To How You React To People

It is always better to respond instead of reacting to any situation. Reactions are involuntary, while a response is a deliberate and voluntary act. For instance, when you touch something hot, you react. Reactions can help life-threatening situations, but if you allow these reactions to get the better of your logical and analytical mind, you can never regulate your emotions. As a manager, you are constantly interacting with different individuals. When you learn to respond, you have time to rationally observe the situation, calculate your response, and make the best decision with the available information.

Become Mindful Of How You Feel

When you are busy moving from one responsibility to another while meeting deadlines and dealing with external demands, you might lose touch with your emotions. This increases the risk of reacting unconsciously. By doing this, you are effectively missing out on valuable information that can help with better decision-making. Any emotional reaction you have offers information about a specific circumstance, person, or even situation. When you pay attention to how you feel, it becomes easier to manage something. After all, how can you deal with something that you are not even aware of?

Become Mindful Of Your Behaviour

Make a note of all the emotions you experience and identify how it influences your daily life. Do your emotions regulate your communication skills? Do they improve or reduce your overall productivity and sense of wellbeing? Ask yourself these questions to improve your behaviour and prevent emotions from regulating it.

Learn To Identify Your Emotions Correctly

After this, you need to take responsibility for your emotions, feelings, and behaviours. It is relatively easy to blame others for these things. This is a mistake most of us are guilty of making. If you always look for others or situations to blame, you will never fully control or regulate your emotions. Without this, you cannot improve your emotional intelligence. Whatever happens might not always be in your control. Still, you have complete control over how you feel about the situation, the emotions you experience, and how you react or behave in such situations. Since you can control this, you can effectively change the course of action you take.

While At Work, Learn To Maintain A Positive Environment

This is an integral part of your managerial role. Apart from this, do the same thing in your personal life, too. By creating and maintaining a healthy and positive atmosphere, you will automatically feel better about yourself. Whether it is spending time with your loved ones or engaging in activities you love, make time for it. By creating a positive environment, maintaining a positive attitude becomes easier.

It was repeatedly mentioned that managers need to be empathetic. This empathy is not restricted to others and should be extended toward yourself. Do not be harsh, judgmental or overly critical of yourself. You are your worst enemy. It is easy to criticise yourself for every mistake you make. If you constantly put yourself down, criticise all your actions, and do not celebrate your victories, it will slowly but surely eat away at your self-confidence. Avoid doing this to improve your emotional intelligence. Become mindful of your internal dialogue and ensure that it does not take on a gloomy hue.

Dealing With Burnout As A Manager

In the previous chapter, you learned managers need to be vigilant at the workplace to identify feelings of burnout and disengagement within their team. Even you are a human being, and if you are not careful, the risk of burnout increases. The good news is that you have complete control over this specific area of your life.

Here are some practical tips you can use to reduce the risk of burnout.

There's Nothing Wrong With Prioritising Your Work Life

The real trouble starts when you have no time or energy to concentrate on your personal life and responsibilities. By maintaining a proper work-life balance, you can make the most of the resources available. It also increases your overall productivity. Therefore, it is time to take a break from your work and schedule regular social activities. Regardless of how hectic your job gets, do not let it become the only thing you do in life. Unless you make a conscious effort to schedule regular social activities, you will never find the time to do so. How do you feel after spending time with your loved ones after a tiring and hectic day? Chances are you feel quite good and relaxed. Whether it is watching movies, playing games, going on trips together, or even just talking, all these things are fun. Make time for fun, and do not get overwhelmed by your professional responsibilities.

Do You Have A Specific Hobby Or Passion?

Is your busy schedule preventing you from working on these things? If yes, it's time to change things a little. If there are no hobbies that you want to pursue, there's no time like the present to learn something new. When you follow your passion, your self-satisfaction will increase. When you are satisfied with your life, the chances of burnout are reduced. This ensures you have a positive attitude toward your work and other responsibilities. Indulging in your hobbies helps you take a break from the weekly grind.

If You Don't Want To Burn Yourself Out, Pay Attention To Your Physical, Mental, And Emotional Health

The simplest way to take care of all these things is by following a healthy diet, adding sufficient exercise to your daily routine, and getting enough sleep at night. Even if one of these three aspects of your life is out of balance, it adversely affects everything else. Since you have complete control over your diet, exercise pattern, and sleep, take positive action today. Consume healthy and wholesome meals and avoid unhealthy foods. Sleep for at least 7 hours with no disturbance at night and exercise for at least 20 minutes daily. When you take care of your health, you automatically feel better about yourself.

Learn To Be Grateful For All The Good You Have In Life

Chances are, there are things in your life now that you wish for. It could be something as simple as the manager's job you are looking forward to. Now take a moment and be grateful for it. Instead of living your life wishing for things you don't have and making yourself miserable about it, practice gratitude. Every day spends at least 5 minutes being grateful for all the good you have. Start maintaining a gratitude journal. List out three simple things that you cherish and are extremely happy about. Whether it is a job you like, a beloved pet, a healthy relationship, or even a good meal, there is a lot to be grateful for. Once you live your life by practising gratitude, you automatically feel better about yourself. It helps cultivate an abundance mindset instead of a scarcity one.

You Don't Have To Do Everything On Your Own

Remember this in any profession and in your personal life. If you think you need some help with some aspect of your life, don't hesitate. Do not let your ego prevent you from asking for help when you need it. If you are overwhelmed by responsibilities, struggling to accomplish tasks, and it feels like something is weighing heavily on you, reach out to others. Asking for help will make it easier to find acceptable and practical solutions to your problems and reduce the risk of burnout.

Learn To Say No

Saying no is a sign of self-respect and confidence. Were you ever stuck in situations that you could have easily avoided had you said no? If so, now is the time to follow this simple bit of advice. Saying no helps identify your boundaries. Your boundaries define what is and is not acceptable to you. It ensures that you don't burn yourself out.

Self-Management

Self-management is the act or process of controlling yourself and managing your priorities and time. It is the ability to prioritise your goals, accept your actions' responsibility, hold yourself accountable for taking the action to achieve goals, and decide a course of action today.

Here are some self-management suggestions you can follow.

Start Living Your Life Based On Your Core Values.

Your core values can include different things like honesty, honour, acceptability, responsibility, leadership, integrity, challenge, autonomy, authenticity, compassion, competency, creativity, faith, fun, growth, human, influence, loyalty, optimism, pleasure, recognition, respect, spirituality, wisdom, and so on. The list of core values can be endless. Once you live your life based on these core values, there will be no internal conflict. For instance, if you say or do things that contradict one of your core values, it creates inner turmoil. This internal turmoil can manifest into stress that prevents you from leading a healthy or happy life. It also increases ambiguity in what you say and creates discord between your words and actions.

Stand Up For Yourself And All That You Believe In.

Even if you don't have the majority of support on your side, standing up for yourself is a sign of self-respect. No one can do it for you unless you are willing to speak out. Others cannot read your mind regardless of how fantastic your idea or thoughts are.

Do Not Break Your Promises.

Whenever you make a promise, ensure that you keep it and do not break your promises. Honouring your commitments increases trust, faith, and confidence others have in you. Your actions will speak louder than your words when you do this.

Break Free Of Any Unproductive Or Bad Habits You Have.

Replace them with healthier and more productive attitudes and practices. To do this, you need to take a long, hard look at your life and all the different things you wish to change. Good habits increase your positive momentum to keep going in life, while bad habits drain your energy. The good news is that you have complete control over habit regulation.

Accept Your Responsibility.

And hold yourself accountable for your actions and behaviours. No one can force you to do things. You always have a choice, regardless of how the situation seems. Therefore, learn to hold yourself accountable for all your behaviours. If you want more responsibility, your accountability also increases. It is not only essential to take credit for all the good you do, but for things that don't go the way you want them to.

Personal Discipline.

Practice the different tips and techniques that were discussed in the previous section to increase your discipline. Without personal discipline, growth and development become distant goals.

Be Nice To Yourself And Others.

Learn to be respectful, courteous, polite, and gracious. Good manners count for a lot in life. Your accomplishments and success cannot be a replacement for good manners.

Maintain a healthy and positive attitude about your work and life. When you start your day on a good note, this momentum keeps you going. There will be bad days, too. But you should not let them weigh heavily on you and prevent you from moving forward. Do not accept a victim mentality. You always have a choice and do not choose to be a martyr or a victim. Learn to choose without regret and always look forward. Do not get stuck living in the past and instead look forward to a brighter and happier future.

CONCLUSION

In this book, you were given all the information you need to transition seamlessly into your new role as a manager. It was filled with helpful tips and advice you can use to become an excellent manager. By letting go of a fixed mindset and adopting a growth mentality, you can concentrate on personal and professional development while ensuring your team's wellbeing. As a manager, you need to play several roles. From a mentor to a coach and a leader, becoming a manager is a full-time responsibility. You are not only responsible for your team's actions, but for their personal development and growth, too. By creating a relationship based on mutual trust, respect, and understanding, you can create an efficient team.

Use the information given in this book to select a managerial style that fits your personality and your team's needs. You need to spend sufficient time and understand all the employees you will manage to do this. After you are comfortable with a specific management style, you need to create an efficient and effective team. The first step to doing this is to lie down the roots for effective, open, and honest communication. Whether it is on social media or face-to-face interactions, unless effective, open, and honest communication exists, you cannot create a workspace environment based on trust and respect.

As a manager, your team depends on and looks up to you for guidance, support, and help. Whether it is a crisis or regular work, your team needs you. Therefore, step up and be a manager your team can look up to. You need to be a good role model too. As a team leader, you need to help your team grow, develop, and ensure they stay involved in the organisation's processes. As a manager, it is your responsibility to instruct and explain, delegate and support, mentor and coach, and motivate and inspire your team members. Once you perform all these tasks effectively, you can improve your team's performance. It also creates better team engagement.

You are the coach, leader, motivator, and trainer for the employees you are managing. Therefore, it is your responsibility to build positive team dynamics, manage employee conflicts, deal with change, and cultivate a high-performance team. To do this, you need to understand how to manage, lead, and motivate your team members and employees. Another vital role that managers play concerning human resource management includes hiring and interviewing potential employees, disciplining employees, firing people, and conducting employee appraisals and interviews. Apart from this, you need to have the personal skills required to manage conflict within the team and employees effectively.

Don't get so carried away with your professional responsibilities that you ignore your personal development. When you are not managing your team or business, focus on developing yourself. Remember, you need to grow and develop as an individual and professional to set a good example for your team to follow. Learn to manage your feelings, work on personal discipline, and improve your emotional intelligence. Self-management and preventing burnout are important for your personal and professional wellbeing.

This book contains all the information you need to become an excellent manager. The different tips, helpful suggestions, and practical advice given in it will teach you about all the things you were probably not taught at management school. This book bridges the gap between theoretical and practical understanding of different responsibilities with the managerial tag.

Now, all that's left for you to do is start implementing the practical tips and suggestions given in this book. During the initial stages, it takes conscious effort. After a while, it will come to you naturally. Also, as you spend more time in a managerial role, you will better understand what it truly means to be a manager. In the meantime, concentrate on improving yourself. Learn to be patient, be an empathetic listener, and regulate your emotions to become the best manager you can be.

ACKNOWLEDGEMENTS

While this book was coming together, I have realised that I was very fortunate to work with and be friends with some fantastic managers throughout my career. A very special thanks to three men who were at the beginning of my managerial journey and who helped me grow and believe that I can always achieve more.

To David - for his friendship, the banter and teaching me to always look for positives.

To Peter - for being my calm, pulling me down to earth when needed and for teaching me about diplomacy.

And to Darren - for always pushing me to be more, do more, and giving me the confidence to try.

Thank you to all the teams I had the privilege of managing. Thank you for your patience, your honesty and for being my dream team. I truly enjoyed working with you, watching you grow, and learning from you.

Finally, a massive thank you to Lukas for his endless patience during this project. It would not happen without his support and faith in my abilities.

REFERENCES

4 Tips For Developing Your Team's Talents. (2013, May 9). CMOE website:
Https://cmoe.com/blog/4-tips-for-developing-your-teams-talents/

5 Ways to Bridge the Generation Gap Between Employees. (n.d.). Engage Blog website:
https://www.achievers.com/blog/5-ways-to-bridge-the-generation-gap-between-employees/

7 Employee Training Tips for Managers | MTI Business Solutions. (n.d.).
training.mtibusiness.com website:
Https://training.mtibusiness.com/content/7_employee_training_tips_for_managers

8 Transition Tips For New Managers | Your Training Edge ®. (n.d.).
Https://www.yourtrainingedge.com/8-transition-tips-for-new-managers/

10 Types of Management Styles: Which One is the Best [2020]. (n.d.). Valamis website:
https://www.valamis.com/hub/management-styles

Baker, M. (2020, April 2). 9 Tips for Managing Remote Employees. www.gartner.com
website: https://www.gartner.com/smarterwithgartner/9-tips-for-managing-remote-employees/

Blakely-Gray, R. (2019, March 29). How to Build a High-performing Team: 6 Tips. Patriot
Software for Small Business website: https://smallbusiness.patriotsoftware.com/build-high-performing-team-steps/

Boettege, E. (2019, October 17). 9 Tips for Managing Conflict in the Workplace. Retrieved
from BizLibrary website: Https://www.bizlibrary.com/blog/self-development/9-tips-for-dealing-with-disagreement-and-conflict/

Brady. (2017, August 6). How To Avoid Managing Like a Dictator: the Value of Teamwork. BNG Team website: Https://www.bngteam.com/blog/avoid-managing-like-dictator-value-teamwork/

Brearley, B. (2017, May 10). 6 Great Ways to Support Your Team - ThoughtfulLeader.com. ThoughtfulLeader.com website: https://www.thoughtfulleader.com/ways-to-support-your-team/

DeakinCo. (2017, December 8). 6 strategies for managing and improving team dynamics. Deakinco.com website: https://www.deakinco.com/media-centre/news/6-strategies-for-managing-and-improving-team-dynamics

Grossman, D. (2020, December 16). 6 Tips to Help Employees Grow and Develop. www.yourthoughtpartner.com website: https://www.yourthoughtpartner.com/blog/bid/73916/6-tips-to-help-employees-grow-and-develop

Half, R. (2016, October 13). How to Manage Organizational Politics. Retrieved from Roberthalf.com website: https://www.roberthalf.com/blog/management-tips/how-to-manage-organizational-politics

Harkless, G. (n.d.). How to Control the Workplace Dynamics Without Becoming a Dictator. Rescue a CEO website: https://rescue.ceoblognation.com/2020/01/18/how-to-control-the-workplace-dynamics-without-becoming-a-dictator/

Heryati, R. (2018, January 30). Why Employee Motivation Is Important (& How to Improve It). The 6Q Blog website: https://inside.6q.io/employee-motivation-important/

How to Manage a New Team. (2017, November). Business News Daily website: https://www.businessnewsdaily.com/10364-managing-new-team.html

Kasey Fleisher Hickey. (2014, December 15). How transparency at work can help your team. Wavelength by Asana website: https://wavelength.asana.com/workstyle-transparency/

Kittaneh, F. (2018, October 11). 3 Tips for Leaders to Improve Their Emotional

Intelligence. Inc.com website: Https://www.inc.com/firas-kittaneh/3-tips-for-leaders-to-improve-their-emotional-intelligence.html

Kurter, H. L. (n.d.). 4 Ways You Can Build Influence And Succeed As A New Manager. Forbes website: https://www.forbes.com/sites/heidilynnekurter/2020/08/28/4-ways-you-can-build-influence-and-succeed-as-a-new-manager/?Sh=5826fd0d5f30

Kwak, J. (n.d.). 3 Keys to Coaching and Mentoring Employees in the Workplace. GoSkills.com website: https://www.goskills.com/Resources/Coaching-and-mentoring-employees-in-the-workplace

Overcoming Employee Resistance To Change In The Workplace. (2016). Paycor.com website: https://www.paycor.com/resource-center/change-management-in-the-workplace-why-do-employees-resist-it

Performance Review Tips for Managers | Monster.com. (2011, February 22). Monster Employer Resources | Monster.com website: Https://hiring.monster.com/employer-resources/workforce-management/employee-performance/performance-management/

Reh, J. (2019, August 28). Supervisors and Managers, Learn to Give Directions to Your Employees. The Balance Careers website: https://www.thebalancecareers.com/how-to-provide-directions-to-your-team-members-2276047

Rowe, A. (n.d.). 5 Ways to Keep Employees on Task Throughout the Day. www.corporatewellnessmagazine.com website: Https://www.corporatewellnessmagazine.com/article/5-ways-to-keep-employees-on-task-throughout-the-day

Rules of Using Humor in Personnel Management. (n.d.). clevercontrol.com website: Https://clevercontrol.com/rules-using-humor-personnel-management

Simonds, S. (2010, March 10). 11 Simple Ways To Avoid Burnout. Lifehack website: Https://www.lifehack.org/articles/featured/11-simple-ways-to-avoid-burnout.html

Stanley, B. (n.d.). 7 Tips on How to Build Effective Teams. ProSky - Learn Skills, Do Projects, Get Hired by Amazing Companies. website:

https://talkingtalent.prosky.co/articles/7-tips-on-how-to-build-effective-teams

Wolf, K. D. (n.d.). How to Tell if Your Team is Burnt Out—and What to do About It. The Muse website: https://www.themuse.com/advice/how-to-tell-if-your-team-is-burnt-outand-what-to-do-about-it.

Wong, K. (2018, January 30). 12 Must-Have Qualities of a Manager | Engage Blog. Engage Blog website: https://www.achievers.com/blog/12-traits-make-great-manager/

Zidle, M. (2011, July 19). 10 Tips for Effective Delegation - Supervision. Supervision website: https://managementhelp.org/blogs/supervision/2011/07/19/10-tips-for-effective-delegation/

ABOUT THE AUTHOR

M. J. Pontus is an experienced manager also an entrepreneur with professional competencies and expertise in the hospitality industry. Since she ventured into the hospitality industry 15 years ago, Magdalena has served in management positions in renowned companies in London, where she has left a lasting legacy through her exemplary performance. She is very vibrant in the management field, and she is ever committed to offering her knowledge to aid people in achieving their career ambitions.

Besides her management proficiency emanating from her management roles, M. J. is also an avid writer. In her first work, Management for Beginners, she has shared her management knowledge to help novice and veteran managers become effective managers in different businesses.

According to M. J., becoming an excellent manager does not happen overnight; it is instead an endless, cumbersome journey where you walk with people all the way. That is why in this book, she has partly given a tribute to all the teams she has worked with, as well as her mentors, whom she is indebted for shaping her management skills.

M. J. is passionate about helping people to thrive in their spheres of influence, especially in the corporate world. More books from M. J., including those about management aspects, are in the pipeline.

SHARE YOUR THOUGHTS

I hope you enjoyed the book. I would love for you to share your thoughts about it:

https://bit.ly/MFBBook

Or you can connect with me directly via:

- My website   https://www.mjpontus.com
- Facebook   https://www.facebook.com/mjpontus
- Instagram   https://www.instagram.com/mjpontus

M. J. Pontus

.

Printed in Great Britain
by Amazon

14687157R00132